Unfuck Your Boundaries

BUILD BETTER RELATIONSHIPS THROUGH CONSENT, COMMUNICATION, AND EXPRESSING YOUR NEEDS

FAITH G. HARPER,
PhD, LPC-S, ACS, ACN

MICROCOSM PUBLISHING
Portland, Ore

UNFUCK YOUR BOUNDARIES

Build Better Relationships through Consent, Communication, and Expressing Your Needs

Part of the 5 Minute Therapy Series
© Dr. Faith Harper, 2016, 2020
This edition © Microcosm Publishing, 2020
First edition, first published 2016
Second edition, first published Jan 14, 2020

ISBN 978-1-62106-616-3
This is Microcosm #291
Illustrations by Trista Vercher
Book design by Joe Biel

For a catalog, write or visit:
Microcosm Publishing
2752 N Williams Ave.
Portland, OR 97227
www.Microcosm.Pub

To join the ranks of high-class stores that feature Microcosm titles, talk to your local rep: In the U.S. **Como** (Atlantic), **Fujii** (Midwest), **Book Travelers West** (Pacific), **Manda/UTP** in Canada, **Turnaround** in Europe, **New South** in Australia, and **GPS** in other countries.

If you bought this on Amazon, I'm so sorry because you could have gotten it cheaper and supported a small, independent publisher at **Microcosm.Pub**

Global labor conditions are bad, and our roots in industrial Cleveland in the 70s and 80s made us appreciate the need to treat workers right. Therefore, our books are MADE IN THE USA and printed on post-consumer paper.

Library of Congress Control Number:2019942377
Names: Harper, Faith G., author.
Title: Unfuck your boundaries : build better relationships through consent, communication, and expressing your needs / by Faith G. Harper.
Description: Second edition. | Portland, Ore : Microcosm Publishing, 2020. | Series: Microcosm ; #199
Identifiers: LCCN 2019021973 (print) | LCCN 2019981509 (ebook) | ISBN 9781621061007 (paperback) | ISBN 9781621060673 (ebook)
Subjects: LCSH: Interpersonal relations. | Interpersonal communication. | Sexual consent. | Expression (Philosophy)
Classification: LCC HM1106 .H3685 2020 (print) | LCC HM1106 (ebook) | DDC 302--dc23
LC record available at https://lccn.loc.gov/2019021973
LC ebook record available at https://lccn.loc.gov/2019981509

MICROCOSM·PUBLISHING

Microcosm Publishing is Portland's most diversified publishing house and distributor with a focus on the colorful, authentic, and empowering. Our books and zines have put your power in your hands since 1996, equipping readers to make positive changes in their lives and in the world around them. Microcosm emphasizes skill-building, showing hidden histories, and fostering creativity through challenging conventional publishing wisdom with books and bookettes about DIY skills, food, bicycling, gender, self-care, and social justice. What was once a distro and record label was started by Joe Biel in his bedroom and has become among the oldest independent publishing houses in Portland, OR. We are a politically moderate, centrist publisher in a world that has inched to the right for the past 80 years.

CONTENTS

Introduction

Our boundaries are the essential building blocks of our relationships. They are how we operate in the world. They are our rules of engagement. Our everyday expressions of consent. The space in which we navigate relationships and community. Really, that's it in a nutshell.

Boundaries are the literal structure of how we live in the world. Which means that understanding them is fundamental, needful information for being a human. It should be a class in kindergarten and every grade after.

So why are conversations about boundaries devalued and diminished? Why are they made fun of? Why is the idea of standing up for our space in the world met with derision?

Healthy boundaries are as much about social justice as interpersonal effectiveness. If we don't have boundaries, we are as malleable as play-doh. And if we are malleable, we are controllable. Boundary violations may not even be overtly awful things that are happening to us. It could be the day to day chipping away at our personhood with things that are "okay."

(I mean, how many times have you said, *"It's okay,"* but it actually wasn't good, or healthy, or wanted, and piece after piece of you disappeared?)

But what if we took it all back? What if we said, serious as a heart attack, that discussions around boundaries aren't whiny bullshit but instead are the blueprint to saving ourselves and our relationships, for moving from "okay" to healthy, good, and strong?

I wanna do that. Do you wanna do that with me? Because, fair warning, this isn't an avo toast level of book. If you have read my other stuff, you know I talk about boundaries almost as much as I talk about trauma. But I am hearing, over and over, that people want to take a deeper dive into their work around boundaries. So that's where this book came from.

This is the serious heavy lifting of conversations around topics like #metoo and #timesup. Around coercive control as a far more insidious and harmful form of abuse in relationships than violence. Around dysfunctional family systems. And people pleasing. And cultural norms that tell you to be polite.

Boundaries help us feel safer and more secure in a world that is usually anything but. They are our foundational supports for existence. Having healthy boundaries means understanding where we need space and where we need scaffolding. It means communicating those needs to the people around us.

Instead, in modern culture, boundaries are more often defined by a lack of words or actions. Not talking about things sends the message that these things *aren't worth talking about*. That they don't matter. That what we want, need, and desire doesn't matter. That who we are in relation to others doesn't matter. And that seeps into *all* our other interactions.

And it also needs to be said (I mean not to *you* because *you* get it...but for some of the folks in the back) that boundaries aren't a tool of manipulation. They aren't a mechanism for controlling other people and having them bow to your will. Boundaries are about claiming your own space, not claiming other people's space.

If boundaries are a relational foundation, and you realize that your foundation needs some work, putting in some support beams now may help prevent a catastrophe later. So many people are afraid that expressing their boundaries will push others away or force others to act against their own will. Generally, the opposite is true. When we do not set and maintain boundaries, we end up resentful and withdrawn from relationships and *that* is what leads to their eventual breakdown.

So where do we start setting positive, healthy boundaries? Boundaries are inherently unique to each person and there is no one-size-fits-all way to manage them. But we can create a framework for discussion. We can look at ourselves and start conversations that we haven't had before. And this has the power to create huge shifts not just in our lives, but within the rest of the world.

This isn't just self-changing work, it's world-changing work.

Let's get to it.

What You'll Find in this Book

Ever seen two tiny people end up having a really big kid? This book had two small parents... the original boundaries zine which was really popular; and a couple of the chapters from my book *Unfuck Your Intimacy*, which focused on boundaries and communication in romantic relationships. So many people have asked for more on this topic, that I rewrote those sections and included them within a bigger framework around boundaries as its own thang. So now what you have in your hands is my big-assed boundaries baby. And here is what this particular baby is all about:

Firstly, I am going to get up into my Professor Faith role and define boundaries, talk about the different types and styles of boundaries and the different kinds of boundary violations. And also, because I just can't help myself, there is some info on the brain science of boundaries. It's a new field so there isn't a ton, but it's interesting (not to mention relevant as fuck to everything else we're talking about).

Then there's the hard part of the book. We are going to really look at how and why are boundaries get so fucked up to begin with. Societal messages, trauma, and attachment, ways of relating in the world. 0% fun but 100% important.

Then. *Then*. If you are still hanging in with me, we will use all that information to talk about all of the important work around boundary unfuckening. Learning to become more aware of our boundaries and how they are respected (or completely disrespected) by others. Plus a ton on communication. Communication is so much about boundary negotiation, isn't it? And holy shit, it's so hard to do well. So I'm gonna share all my favorite communication tools and tricks for far less than the cost of a therapy session with me.

Finally, because boundary violations at their extreme worst involve abuse to our personhood, there's a whole list of resources in the back of the book to help you find ways to either get out of or stay safe in violent relationships.

And because y'all are proactive badasses who are here to tackle shit head-on, I've sprinkled in some grounding, mindful-y type exercises throughout the book, because tackling shit head-on is fucking activating. Paying attention to the fact that this is really difficult, and taking care of yourself in the process is important. Because boundaries are a moot point if you are a puddle of emotional goo crying on the bathroom floor. And goo can't change the world, which is what we are all setting out to do.

And if workbooks help you live your best life (or if you are running boundaries workshops or similar awesome endeavors, check out the *Unfuck Your Boundaries Workbook*. It works just fine on its own or in conjunction with the book you currently have in hand.

What Are Boundaries?

L et's start with a pragmatic discussion about boundaries.

The term boundary really just refers to the line (literal or metaphorical) that marks the limits of a particular area. Boundaries are the edge territory of what belongs to us and what belongs to someone else.

Boundaries within any relationship, intimate or otherwise, can take many forms. They range from sexual issues (*"No butt stuff, stop pressuring me!"*) to privacy issues (*"Stay out of my journal, FFS!"*) to just everyday interactions (*"Please don't come by my desk and chat with me today, I'm behind on that project and I'm terrible at multitasking"* or *"I need twenty minutes to decompress when I get home from work"*).

Boundaries aren't just the hard nos, they are also the maybes and the yesses-with-limits. Like, *"Please knock before coming into my room,"* or *"I'm not sure if I want to attend that event, let me see if this pain flare dissipates by Friday."*

Additionally, boundaries change over time, across situations, and within different relationships. There isn't a specific trig formula you can apply in all situations that makes this easy. And any guru-type person who says otherwise is 103% full of shit. If it were all so super-simple, we wouldn't be having these conversations. I would be writing books about my cats or something. Definitely not trying to corral everything I have learned and shared about boundaries throughout my years of clinical practice into something actually usable.

Types of Boundaries

I t can be helpful to think of boundaries as having seven main categories:

Physical Boundaries: These are the boundaries that deal with the pragmatics of touch (when, where, how, who, etc.)—both of others touching you and you touching others.

Property Boundaries: These are the boundaries that deal with the things we own or lay claim to. Our homes, bikes, favorite t-shirts. Of course, our primal little brains can get us into trouble in this regard, as well. People will decide that a chair in a classroom or conference room is "theirs" and no-one else should sit in it. And I have caught myself taking personal offense that someone else purchased that last ginger cookie *right fucking in front of me because they totally knew I wanted it and they are trying to* *hurt me.* Ahem. Humans definitely have territorial issues, don't we?

Sexual Boundaries: Sexual boundaries include the physical and emotional aspects of sex. They also cover information about our sexual selves: Who we like, what we like to do with the people we like, etc. They're about acceptable language, ideas, and information around sexuality. They're about terms you use surrounding sex and if jokes about sex are funny or offensive to you. Sex is such an important part of most people's lives that our boundaries around sex are *way* bigger than the sexual acts we engage in.

Emotional-Relational Boundaries: Emotional-relational boundaries are not just about how we want to feel and how others want to feel. They are even more about demonstrating our respect for our own personhood and the personhood of others. We respect these boundaries through how we care for others and by letting them have their own emotional experiences. But also, they are about not taking responsibility for other people's emotions (because we've all dealt with someone in a raunchy mood who tried to release that pressure valve onto us).

Intellectual Boundaries: Intellectual boundaries are about our thoughts, beliefs, and ideas and how they are respected. They are also about our access to information, ideas, and opportunities to learn. They are separate from emotional boundaries because someone can be emotionally kind (sorta) but not respect your worldview. And someone can think you are brilliant and wise, but still treat you like shit in other ways.

Spiritual Boundaries: Spiritual boundaries are about our belief systems, how we practice them, and what we choose to share around these beliefs. This is different from intellectual boundaries because spirituality is our human experience of purposeful belonging. It's a self-in-relation to something bigger than our own emotional and intellectual experiences, and that can be a point of bigger vulnerability for many people. Spiritual boundary violations could take the form of forcing someone to pray who doesn't want to, or not letting someone pray who does want to.

Time Boundaries: These are boundaries regarding one of our most precious resources: the expenditure of our minutes, hours, and days. There are plenty of things that I'm super interested in doing and that don't cross my intellectual, emotional, or other types of boundaries, but I don't have the physical time to invest in them. You totally know what I mean by that, you've been there, too, right?

There is a lot of overlap between these categories. A fairly simple boundary violation could be tied to just one category. The person who whacks your ankle with their shopping cart at the grocery store? Simple physical boundary violation. Or multiple boundaries can be pushed at once. Someone asking for your help with a project is potentially running into both your intellectual and time boundaries, right? And possibly some emotional ones, too.

And maybe that complexity of experience is what makes the whole conversation so hard. It makes figuring out our boundaries and trying to communicate about them better so complicated. Because it high-key *is* complicated. But hey, as the author Glennon Doyle says *"We can do hard things."* And this is a worthwhile endeavor.

Questions for Consideration

1) What are some of the boundaries that you have for each of these categories?

2) Which kinds of boundary violations do you experience the most? Which categories do those violations belong in?

3) Which kinds of boundaries do you have the most difficulty respecting for others? Which categories do those violations belong?

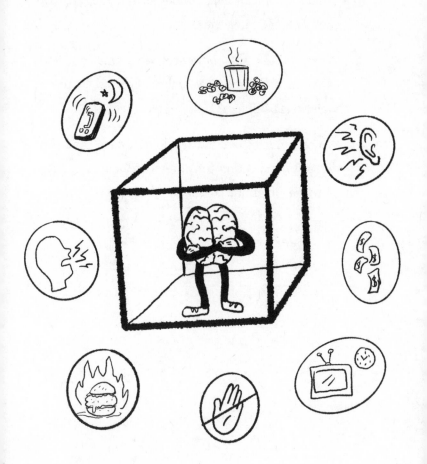

How Our Boundaries Are Defined

Besides having different types of boundaries, we also have the structure of the boundaries themselves to consider...which is more important than most people realize. Boundaries can be rigid, permeable, or flexible.

While some people have set up camp in one of these categories, most of us will operate on a continuum of these in different situations.

Rigid Boundaries are boundaries that nothing gets through, ever, and there is zero space for negotiation. Some boundaries should be rigid AF. I mean, my boundaries around not having people punch me in the face or empty my bank account are rigid because they should be. But not all boundaries need to be that hardcore. Like, you know how some people go to bed pretty early (and by some people, I mean me...) so they (me) don't like to be called after 9 pm? If our boundaries are super rigid in general, or super rigid around a particular issue that means we are absolutely *not* having any phone calls after 9 pm. Our phone is off or we don't answer it or whatever. You can't get ahold of us if it's past 8:59, which could definitely end up with some downsides for us.

Permeable Boundaries are ones that everything gets through if it wants to. These boundaries are defined for you. Attacks come from the outside, and you don't know how to hold your ground. So if I kept answering my phone when it rings late at night and having long, drawn-out conversations when I should be sleeping, my boundary around that is permeable. Meaning, I let people do whatever they want in a particular situation. Generally speaking, permeable boundaries is just code for "letting people walk all over you." But sometimes, some boundaries should be permeable, just like sometimes, some boundaries should be rigid. For example, in my therapy office, my life is easiest if people sit on the sofa and I sit in my comfy saucer chair. But we aren't there to make *my* life easier, we are there for therapy. So people can sit whatever the fuck they want (yes, including in my comfy saucer chair) and I will follow suit. I have sat on the floor with many people because that's what they needed.

Flexible Boundaries are the baby-bear middle ground that we should operate from for most of our boundary situations. Flexible boundaries are the ones that come from listening to our internal voice that wants to protect us *and* wants us to experience growth. That's the voice that makes continuous calibrations about our boundaries, knowing that when we are willing to compromise in certain areas it may lead to the betterment of the relationship and emotional growth for yourself. Back to the middle-aged lady who goes to bed early: I have a son who lives and works in a different time zone and is literally unable to call before 9 pm. Middle-aged lady happens to really like her son and is delighted that a busy, grown-ass man still likes to check in with his mom now and then. So if he calls and she's not conked out yet, she answers and they have a lovely chat for a few minutes. Flexible boundaries FTW.

Some boundaries should be rigid if they defend real safety and security. These are the boundaries that reflect needs rather than wants. And some rigid boundaries apply to everyone. Not attacking people with no provocation, for example.

Most are not so universal. Boundaries that are rigid for me may not be an issue at all for someone else. For instance, someone who is neurodiverse may need more alone time than other people. Someone with a trauma history may never feel comfortable with certain sexual positions. We have all had different experiences and have different needs based on them. That's part of the human condition. Our boundaries also change in different relationships, different circumstances, and different points in our lives.

I'm guessing you picked up this book because you think your boundaries are too permeable. That's the most common problem most of us face with boundaries. When message after message reinforces the notion that our boundaries have no value and are not worthy of respect, we internalize that message. And even as we mature into situations where we have more control over our surroundings, we don't know how to exercise that control.

So we need to learn to firm up our boundaries, but baby bear style. Not too hard and not too soft.

Overly rigid boundaries can also be a response to past experiences, a form of overcorrection for boundaries that were too permeable in the past. For example, refusing to go on a date with anyone ever after being victimized by a romantic partner. We are the product of all our experiences, and if we had some pretty fucked up ones in the past, it entirely makes sense to overcorrect in order to protect ourselves in the present and future. Overly rigid boundaries may present us with a sense of safety in the short term because they help insulate us from situations that scare us. But that isn't the point of boundaries. Boundaries are designed to provide us safe passage through life, not as a mechanism of controlling every environment we are in and every person we interact with.

If, generally speaking, your boundaries are very strict, I'm totally *not* telling you to stop having boundaries. But I'm definitely saying that building ridiculous walls around yourself in the name of boundaries is going to keep you from living a full life just as much as having no boundaries at all. And honestly, being a rigid asshole is just as bad for us in the long run as letting someone stomp all over us.

With all boundaries, we need the capacity to negotiate while still maintaining our safety and not becoming a total pushover. It's that nebulous, hard-to-define difference between flexibility and permeability. For example, maybe you are starting back to school after not being in that headspace for some time. You may have to set up really rigid boundaries with others about your study time because you are feeling overwhelmed and easily distracted. But as you get into the groove of completing your coursework, you may be more open to others being in the room with you while you're studying, don't mind taking a phone call, etc. Or if you're the person who swore you'd never date again, you might be willing to go out with someone who has been vetted by a trusted friend so long as you can meet in a low-stress, easy-to-leave venue like a coffee shop.

There is a term in anthropology called *liminality* which refers to that uncomfortable feeling of being on the threshold between two states, like the past and the future. Leaning into the discomfort of unpacking where our boundaries have been overly permeable and overly rigid allows us to cross into a different way of relating to others. Flexible boundaries mean paying attention in a proactive way instead of reacting from old patterns. And that may mean you have to make some difficult choices. Because when it comes down to it, we either let the world dictate our boundaries for us *or* we communicate them with what we do and say. As off-kilter as it can be at times, I would *far* rather experience the discomfort of difficult conversations than let the world determine what is going to happen to me.

Questions for Consideration

Here are some questions to explore your existing boundaries (whether or not you've started communicating them to others):

- What messages have you internalized about your right to healthy boundaries and the ownership of your individual needs?

- Generally speaking, are the majority of your boundaries rigid, flexible, or permeable?

- Which of your boundaries are rigid right now? Are there any that need to be challenged in that regard? Are there any that need to be more rigid?

- Which of your boundaries are permeable right now? Are there any that need to be challenged and strengthened into being flexible or even rigid? Do you have any boundaries that should remain permeable? If so, how does that permeability support, sustain, or serve you at this point in your life?

- What would your ideal boundary balance look like? How close to this ideal are you right now?

- What is something that is actively in your control that you can work on to move in the direction of your ideal?

Boundary Violations (and Why Consent Is Super Important)

I've defined boundaries as the constructs that differentiate between ourselves and someone else. Boundary violations can occur when that space is not negotiated in conscious and mindful ways and our actions result in harm (regardless of our intentions).

This is very much about consent. Consent is used as a buzzword that confuses a lot of people, but in practice it's a simple concept. Consent is *the informed, voluntary permission given or agreement reached for an activity/ exchange between two or more sentient beings*. When it comes to the expression and negotiation of our boundaries, we generally do so through how we communicate consent. If someone asks you "Hey, can I borrow this book?" they are recognizing that the book is something you own (property boundary!), and are asking for your consent to use it and return it. You are then free to give your consent, not give it, or give it conditionally.

Boundary violations are what happen when we act without consent.

Pia Mellody, author of *Facing Codependence*, points out two main categories of boundary violations. Her categories are, simply enough, external and internal.

1) *External Boundary Violations* are when people do something to you in a physical way. Touching you without your permission. Taking your shit without you agreeing for them to do so. External boundary violations are tangible and measurable.

2) *Internal Boundary Violations* are when people violate your emotional space and try to get you to change your behavior and actions to suit their needs without requesting that change honestly. It's manipulative shit. Sometimes this takes the form of coercive control, which we get into later in the book.

What do boundary violations look like? Sara Hines Martin's book *Shame on You!: Help for Adults from Alcoholic and Other Shame-Bound Families* has an excellent list, which

I adapted and categorized based on Pia Mellody's work. Some of these things are huge, and some are the everyday grievances we all experience, but they are all boundary violations and are important to our discussion.

I'm including a long (exhausting, depressing, and somewhat overwhelming) list of examples of boundary violations on the following pages. This list is an important part of the discussion because so many of the systemic, cultural problems that fuck up our boundaries make it so we don't often realize that boundaries are being violated right and left. That people are violating our boundaries and we are violating other people's boundaries. And yes, we stomp all over our own boundaries when we de-center our own needs in order to appease others.

I tell people on the regular *"when we know better, we do better."* The big cultural shifts start with *recognizing* these violations.

Examples of External Boundary Violations

- Sexual abuse

- Physical abuse

- Unwanted touch (including touch at times someone doesn't want to be touched, in ways they don't want to be touched, and in places the person doesn't want to be touched)

- Entering someone's living space without consent

- Cutting in front of someone in line without consent

- Not cleaning up one's own mess

- Using another person's property without consent

- Not returning or being late to return property (even if it was borrowed with consent)

- Not adhering to time agreements (being perpetually late or uncomfortably early)

- Taking control of someone else's child when their parent or guardian is present

- Moving in to live with another person without permission (IKR? But it happens)

- Smoking in front of others or in their living space without their consent

Examples of Internal Boundary Violations

- Asking personal questions outside of the depth of the relationship

- Asking others to justify their actions or viewpoints when neither impacts us

- Giving feedback about someone's behavior when it doesn't affect us

- Listening to the phone conversations of others

- Reading others' diaries, letters, emails, or private messages

- Sharing secrets or things told to us in confidence (gossiping counts here)

- Assuming the feelings of others

- Assuming the reasons for others' behavior

- Assuming others' thoughts

- Making demands instead of requests

- Expressing "advice" or "constructive criticism" when it was unsolicited and/or is offered for the sole purpose of hurting the person who is the recipient of the comments.

- Treating someone in a condescending way (talking to people as if they were a child or slow to understand)

- Judging others

- Sharing personal information about oneself without checking out if the hear-er wants to hear it

- Using abusive language

- Misgendering someone

- Using transphobic or trans-exclusionary language

- Using racist, or racially stereotyped language

- Asking for excessive or inappropriate favors

- Expecting a favor exchange (giving favors assuming favors will be given in return)

- Triangulating (trying to use a third party to control someone)

Examples of Boundary Violations That Could Be Both Internal and External

- Pushing past someone's "no" or any limits they have set

- Helping someone without first asking if they would like help

- Interrupting someone while they are talking

- Trying to force adults to live by someone else's moral and ethical standards

- Intruding at a gathering, such as joining others at a restaurant without being invited

- Continued pursuit of a relationship with someone who has indicated that they are not interested (regardless if they had maintained a relationship in the past)

- Indulging our desires at the expense or harm of another

One caution as we look at these: There's something all our brains are wired to do called the *fundamental attribution error*. When we mess up and violate someone else's boundaries, we attribute our actions to the situation at hand (whether this is a reasonable justification or not). When other people mess up and violate our boundaries, we attribute it to them being a fundamentally terrible person.

This is the brain's default way of thinking and until we develop an awareness of it and learn how to think through it, we end up being pretty awful to other people and expecting the worst from them. Adding a level of consideration and awareness allows us to pay attention to the details of each situation we encounter and make better decisions about whether someone is a true threat to our safety (and we will be talking more about red flags in that regard later in this book) or just a blundering human that will do better in the future if we bring our issues to their attention.

Questions for Consideration

1) Were there any boundary violations listed that you hadn't really thought of as being boundaries before?

2) Were they internal, external, or both?

3) Are there certain types of boundary violations that you have experienced more often than others historically?

4) What about in the present?

5) Are there certain types of boundary violations that you have been guilty of (even unintentionally) in the past?

6) What about in the present?

7) Are there any other boundary violations that I didn't list here that you have noticed/thought of?

I'm including grounding exercises in this book because unpacking some of our issues around boundaries can be really fucking activating. And hey, if someone recommended this book to you and you realize you are not ready, I get that. Put it aside until you are. Zero judgement... you know you better than anyone else does.

But if you feel that you are ready to do the work, but you know that getting through it is going to be uncomfortable and even painful, grounding exercises are designed to help with that. Grounding only means keeping yourself in the present, when facing up to the past.

Part of how the brain thinks it is keeping us safe is to tell us a story about the past, layering it onto the present so we perceive ourselves as reliving a traumatic situation. It's a great safety mechanism in actual dangerous situations... but it does nothing to help us deal with past issues so we can heal and move forward.

This is a simple exercise for when our brain does this. I encourage everyone to create a grounding statement that reminds them that they are in the present and doing

1) This is only a memory. Memories suck, but they can't hurt me.

2) In the past, I was a victim. Now I am a survivor.

Come up with one that works for you, make a note of it somewhere and use the shit out of it as needed. I also suggest iced coffee as a backup option. Take care of you.

This is Your Brain on Boundaries

The study of boundaries on the brain science level is part of a brand new field of science called neuroethics. *Neuroethics* refers to the overlap between social norms, philosophy, anthropology, and empirical brain science.

Imaging technology is allowing us to see that the boundaries between ourselves, others, and the environment are something that exists in the brain, not just an idea that millennials came up with to piss off boomers.

And, not at all surprising for those of you who have read my book *Unfuck Your Brain*, the part of the brain where these boundaries exist is the amygdala, the area of the brain that processes our emotions and regulates our fear response.

Before I get into the exact science of this, let's review what the amygdala does when it perceives a threat. To do that, we need to revisit the *fight/flight/freeze response*, which is our threat response system. I've talked about this in most of my previous books, but here's a refresher:

- Fight is *beat their ass before your ass gets beat.*

- Flight is *get the fuck up out of here this isn't safe.*

- Freeze is *if you play possum and don't respond at all maybe all this will go away.*

This is crazy important to our survival. This whole process is our emergency broadcast system, replete with electronic beeping in the background.

Here's how it works: our prefrontal cortex, which is the thinking, logical part of our brain, takes in some outside information. Which could be a boundary violation, like someone bumping into us (physical attack?) or hugging us without our consent (lack of respect for body autonomy?). This is why boundary violations in the present can operate as trauma responses to past events.

The amygdala flips through the index of previous similar experiences and if the shittier option was the one that panned out it says, *"I remember that! last time that shit happened, it hurt! hurt sucks!"* And the brain stem tells the prefrontal cortex *"Get the fuck up out of there! We don't like to hurt!"* So we say "Peace out, threatening situation, gotta jet!" Or we fight back. Or freeze up and play dead and hope the situation passes us over.

When this process gets out of hand and the amygdala is on a hair-trigger and freaks out all the time about things that aren't actually a threat, that's a trauma response. *Unfuck Your Brain* is about how to calm it down so it just responds to actual threats again. For now, let's talk more about how our amygdala regulates our boundaries.

About ten years ago, some scientists were working with a woman with a genetic disease known as Urbach-Wiethe, which fucks up the amygdala hardcore. This patient had a serious problem with understanding personal space. So they conducted a study, comparing her comfort level with personal space (a physical boundary) against people who did not have this disease. People without the disease needed twice the distance between themselves and other people than the Urbach-Wiethe lady did. Her brain didn't have that switch that recognized a physical boundary and signaled, *"Whoa, back the fuck up please."*

The scientists said "Whoa, weird shit, here" and did more fMRI scans of the individuals in the study that did not have Urbach-Wiethe and found that the amygdala would light up when the scientists orbited into their personal space zone *even if the individuals couldn't see, hear, or feel them.*

Still with me? This means that the amygdala regulates distance from others even when conscious sensory cues aren't present. It's a survival instinct. So when the brain flags a boundary violation, it invokes a protective, survival-based response, tripping the switch to the sympathetic nervous system. And the sympathetic nervous system? The mechanism that triggers the fight/flight/freeze response.

It's not just something in a Phillip K. Dick novel anymore—we can read people's biological and mental boundaries as a physical entity, not just a philosophical idea. And this research will be hugely beneficial, not just in understanding people with weird and rare diseases, but also in understanding why boundaries are more difficult for a number of people to understand (for example, all y'all neurodiverse rock stars). Which means we can have different, and more pragmatic conversations about them while honoring that they are a very real part of our survival response.

And maybe now you are thinking, okay then, chica...but I'm not walking around with a portable fMRI, so how do I recognize when a boundary violation has lit up my amygdala? Especially if my past experiences in this regard have been pretty fucked up (and yes, so much more on later in this book)? Hey, you're learning to trust yourself again and you gotta start somewhere. Let's look at some ways of doing that, ok?

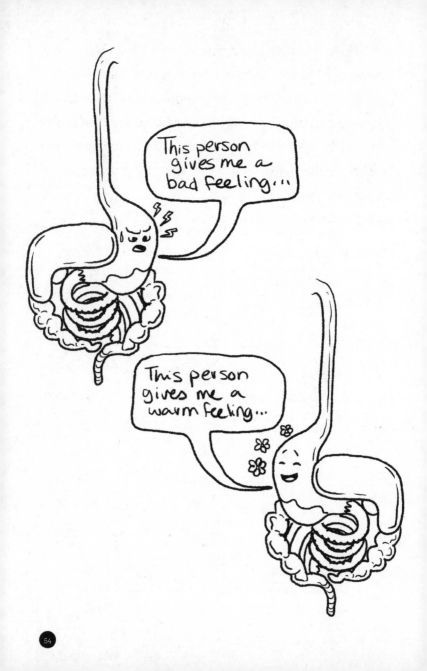

Listening to Your Body

I have heard soooo many people tell me that they only realized a situation was pretty fucked up a while after it happened. I've totally done the same thing, where I responded to something in the moment based on social expectations rather than what my gut was telling me, and realized later that it wasn't okay.

Mr. Dr. Faith is a certified recovery coach working in community mental health. He's also a former private investigator who used to do the most ridiculous and dangerous jobs on the regular. So let's just say his bullshit meter is finely tuned. I asked him recently about his reads on people and how he knows someone is safe or not. He shrugged and said:

"Because the little man who lives in my stomach says so."

If you are wondering what the fuck that story has to do with boundaries the answer is "all the things." Because tuning into our bodies in our day to day interactions is as close as we are going to get to a 24/7 fMRI machine telling us a boundary is being violated.

Here's the thing: our subconscious is attending to far more incoming information than our conscious mind is. The study of information refers to this idea as *compression theory*. In a nutshell, we are taking in 11 million bits of data any given second, but can only consciously attend to about 50 of those bits in the same given second. Data compression (also called compaction) is the process of reducing the amount of information available. If we are compressing a bunch of computer files into a ZIP drive, that's *lossless*...meaning all the original data is still there. In the human brain, it is *lossy* (yes that's the real word), meaning that some information gets lost in the translation process.

The difference between zip drives and human brains is pretty important, right?

Physiologists were also the people to discover that we have a way of compensating for our human data compression process which lies in the body (which is why I got into hypnotherapy to begin with, it connects the entirety of the body with the working subconscious mind). It's our *reflex system*, which kicks in within $1/10^{th}$ of a second of confronting stimulus. These are a lot of science-y terms to explain that we have a reaction with our bodies to what's going on around us, even if the information never gets processed on a conscious level.

At a subconscious level, our body is saying "oh, fuck no" to boundary violations in a very real way, through something called *visceral afferent messaging*. This just means an inward feeling from the body, telling the mind what to do, instead of the mind making a decision telling the body what to do. This information is relayed through the vagus nerve through something called *monoaminergic neurons* (and now you are super ready for bar trivia night!!).

TL;DR? *Gut reactions are real, literal things.*

And since the vagus nerve is involved, these body-based messages are signaling our whole system which is why you may notice things like a racing heart, feeling tearful, chills, difficulty breathing, and other physical markers of fear. Paying attention to the dude that lives in your stomach may save your life and can definitely save you some heartache.

Questions for Consideration

1) How does your body warn you of danger? What do you notice?

2) Consider a situation where your gut instincts told you something and you ignored those instincts? What led you to ignore these instincts?

3) Do you have situations that may have caused faulty wiring regarding your gut instincts? An overactive danger response because of a trauma history? Or were you socially conditioned to *not* listen to your gut growing up? If this is the case, who are your trusted people that you can check-in with to verify if your gut instincts are on point or off-kilter?

How Our Boundaries Get Fucked Up

I f boundaries, consent, and healthy communication were super easy, there would be zero need for this book, right? Like, if we had a culture that supported these skills and we centered teaching them from an early age I quite likely wouldn't have the job that I have.

But instead, this is really difficult, paddling-against-the-flow work. And it's desperately needed. Not just for our day-to-day interactions but for the world overall. And it would be disingenuous to discuss how to unfuck our interactions with others without first discussing how they got fucked to begin with.

There are probably eleventy-billion different reasons that boundaries get smashed to smithereens on the regular. But for the sake of not wanting to write the *Encyclopedia of Boundary Fuckery,* I'm sticking to four of the biggies: overall social hierarchy problems, screwed up attachment styles, high conflict personalities, and the perpetuation of coercive control. I'm focusing on these four because they are the ones that I see people struggling with day in and day out as a therapist. Besides being really common, these are the issues that require examining a lot about how we live as individuals and within a society.

It's not easy. I know how hard this was to write, and I do this work on the regular. So I have a pretty good inkling about how hard it may be for a lot of people to read. And while research shows that trigger warnings are not effective at preventing individuals from experiencing trauma reactions, the least I can do is not sucker punch you with some serious shit. Because coming out the other end of this is how we change the world. And that's the real goal here.

How Society Fucks Up Our Boundaries

O riginally this section focused specifically on sexual violence. The #metoo movement has opened new discussions about gender-based violence and how it has infused all aspects of our culture. And that's important as hell, but centering how cultural issues impact boundary violations solely around sexual violence does a disservice to the bigger issues at play.

(And if you are thinking "I'd kinda like to see what you wrote about sexual violence and #metoo"? All that ended up in my *Unf*ck Your Consent* zine, which is more focused on navigating sexual boundaries, specifically).

The bigger issue, according to the work of social structures scientist Riane Eisler, is that our societies are patterned around what she terms a *dominator model*. In cultures that are structurally maintained in this model, human hierarchies are backed up by the threat of force or actual force.

Another way to think of it is as a *power-over* structure (as opposed to a *power-with* structure). Some humans have power over others, creating a sense of ownership that is continuously reinforced. The dominator model is not just responsible for rape culture, it's responsible for slavery, mass incarceration, lack of access to healthcare by the poor, the horrific mistreatment of political refugees, and all the different ways we deny personhood to whole classes of individuals on a historical and ongoing basis.

And that's an overwhelming realization. Because the next thought is: *Does that mean that all human beings are complete garbage by evolutionary design and we're all just fucked?*

Thank the baby Buddha, no (and I don't think I could ethically do what I do every day if I thought that was true). Humans aren't total shit. Not only do we have the capacity to create more egalitarian social structures, they've always existed. Dr. Eisler calls them *partnership models* and points historically to the !Kung and BaMbuti, and more recently to Scandinavian nations as evidence of our ability to develop the kind of social guidance system that redirects resources to the greater good of all people in society.

Humans have always played an active role in our own social evolution. And this evolution tends to bop along in stasis for long periods of time until we say "fuck this noise" and shake things up (Dr. Eisler would say *"yeah, you mean bifurcation points but whatever"*). Our history is replete with huge systemic, changes in this regard. Look at how the book *The Jungle* by Upton Sinclair changed the rights of laborers in the meatpacking district. Or how Representative John Lewis has impacted civil rights across the past decades.

You've heard the term *consent culture*, right? Consent culture is the normalization of asking for consent for interaction with others. For being disappointed but not butthurt when someone says no. Consent culture at its highest level-up is when we don't feel weird or embarrassed for establishing and respecting boundaries. Our current subcultural shift to consent culture means we are actively and intentionally changing our culture. And as we steer our own evolution, our laws and norms are starting to reflect these ideals.

But overall, we live in a rape culture, not a consent culture. Rape culture is a term that refers to a norm regarding sexual violence. Meaning the general social attitudes and practices tolerate, excuse, condone, and even glamorize sexual violence. We have seen case after case of young men being given light sentences for sexual assault because they had "bright futures" that the judge didn't want to "ruin" (People v. Turner is the biggest recent example). Tolerating, excusing, and condoning right there.

Rape culture is the literal opposite of consent culture. If consent is how we convey boundaries then it's no wonder that rape culture has kneecapped any dialogue or standards of personal boundaries.

In consent culture, only yes means yes. Accepting this means that many people have to revisit past behaviors, to consider that maybe some past actions were actually violations, not "grey areas." Rape culture is essentially a *justification culture*, whereas consent culture means we, all of us, are entirely responsible for our behavior at all times. Power-with instead of power-over, right?

Violence, overall is gendered—men are far more likely to perpetrate violence (against not just women but also other men, non binary individuals, and children than any other demographic group). And sexual assault is the best-studied form of gendered violence, which is why talking about rape culture and consent culture is so powerful. But there are so many other ways that fucked up cultural power dynamics lead to a culture that tolerates systemic boundary violations.

And, yeah, I know. You didn't buy this book for a lesson in political activism and cultural paradigm shifts. You bought it for boundary help. But as Cristien Storm affirms on the very first page in her wonderful book *Empowered Boundaries*, "the very act of boundary setting is political whether we like it or not."

Politics is overwhelming. It's fucking awful and confusing and unending. I understand the desire to disconnect from the political nature of society, and you might be wondering why I am dragging politics into a mental health topic.

In this case, the personal is political. I mean, it always is to a certain extent, but it's hella true here. Respecting boundaries means respecting personhood. And the minute we start saying *"I, too, have a personhood to be respected,"* we are establishing and communicating our boundaries. And by doing that, we are changing our relationships and our expectations of interactions within our surrounding community. We are evolving our concept of consent for the betterment of all humans.

All equal rights movements started with the statement of a boundary. Abolition, voting rights, desegregation, freedom to marry who you love.

When you are recognizing a boundary violation being perpetuated, the first question should be:

Do everyone's boundaries get regularly stomped on like this, or is it just certain people?

Is this a boundary that only women have to fight about? People of color? People who use wheelchairs? People who are not US citizens?

No matter how apolitical you may be in other domains, the minute you start fighting for the establishment and recognition of your boundaries and the boundaries of others you have become a political revolutionary. Welcome to the team.

Questions for Consideration

1) What community/social structures do you operate within that have impacted your ability to articulate your individual boundaries with the expectation of having them respected?

2) Has that changed any as you have gotten older? How so?

3) What kind of response do you anticipate when you challenge these structures?

4) How can you prepare for these anticipated challenges?

5) What's the potential payoff for doing this work?

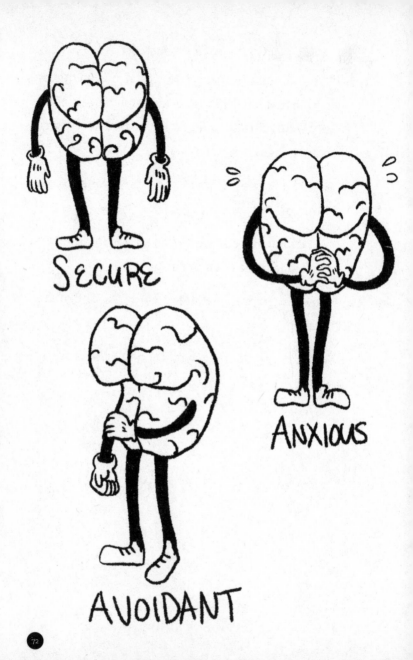

SECURE

ANXIOUS

AVOIDANT

Attachment Styles

O k, it wouldn't be a Dr. Faith book if I didn't start talking about trauma some-damn-where, right?

Even those of us with reasonably privileged upbringings and who have a decent measure of personhood respected in the eyes of the law can really struggle with boundary setting, active consent, and clear communication. We are the product of all of our experiences, right? Not just social norms but what happened to us when we were younger and what continues to happen to us as we settle ourselves into adulthood.

Even really nice and loving parents can still struggle to teach and model healthy communication and boundary setting. And modern educational settings which operate on the need for student compliance aren't going to encourage these kinds of skills either. Many of us with otherwise happy childhoods grew up conflict avoidant or just sheerly ill-equipped to recognize, define, and articulate boundaries in our interactions with others. A lot of that has to do with our larger culture, like I talked about in the last section.

Then there are those of us who are abuse survivors, who often struggle mightily with boundaries in one extreme or another, either not holding them at all or having boundaries so rigid we become completely disconnected from those around us.

Interestingly enough, there are plenty of people who fall in a sort of weird middle space of childhood experiences that weren't totally *Leave It to Beaver* but also not a complete shitshow. Maybe they had parents who loved them but were wrestling with their own demons, and it affected their ability to be a good parent.

Whether abusive or just kinda chaotic, these early experiences affect what therapist types call a*ttachment styles*, which basically just means the dynamics of how we navigate our interpersonal relationships. For many people, their early childhood attachment styles affect their later relationships and how they recognize and establish boundaries with friends, family, and partners.

So let's start with the three attachment styles in a nutshell:

Secure Attachment: Research shows that about 60% of us had secure attachments. (I kinda wonder about this number...like is it really that high? But I'm a trauma therapist so my perspective is skewed, I grant you.) Secure attachment people generally feel comfortable with others. They feel safe depending on someone and having that person depend on them. They don't freak out constantly that they are going to be abandoned or that someone is going to get too close. You know, like generally pretty healthy. Fucking weirdos. Secure attachment people tend to have healthy and flexible boundaries because they have generally found life to not be a scary place to be. They can express what they need with the expectation that that need will be honored, but also don't mind being challenged a little because they expect others to have their best interest and personal growth at heart.

Avoidant Attachment: About 20% of us have an attachment style that is termed avoidant. These are the people who have a hard time trusting or depending on others and are generally uncomfortable with the level of closeness that others want from them. Avoidant attachment people are the ones who are most likely to have pretty rigid boundaries. Their life experiences make their brains scream things like *fuck all these fuckers, they aren't to be trusted.*

Anxious Attachment: The final 20% of us (which you already figured out because you can math) have anxious attachment styles. They often worry that people won't love them or want to be with them or that they are going to scare their partner away. They often crave a closeness with others that they never quite get. Anxious attachment people tend to have more permeable boundaries, as they try to please others by letting themselves be walked over on the regular.

These were the basic categories identified by researchers in the late 70s and early 80s. The attachment styles were first noticed in children and their relationships with their caregivers and were carried forth to adults to see if these attachment styles held true in adult relationships.

These categories make a lot of sense but don't really account for all the different ways these attachment styles actually show up in our day to day lives. Further research in the 90s showed that avoidant and anxious attachments are not necessarily an either/or scenario. To complete the fuckery, some people experience *both*. So our attachment responses can look like any of the following:

Which also explains why our boundary type may veer around all crazy sometimes between overly rigid and overly permeable depending on which of our attachment issues are being activated in any particular scenario.

Research does show that there is a moderate correlation between our childhood attachment style and our attachment style as adults. How we start out can play a big role in how we end up. We react based on our past experiences until we learn different skills. Additionally, the kinds of relationships we have as adults can either reinforce or rewire these attachment styles.

(I mean, derp, right.)

So if these attachment styles are carrying over into our adulting, they are informing how we set, enforce, and respect boundaries. If you are responding from an avoidant attachment style, you're far more likely to entrench yourself into some rigid boundaries, but if your attachment style gets into anxious territory, you may find yourself stomping

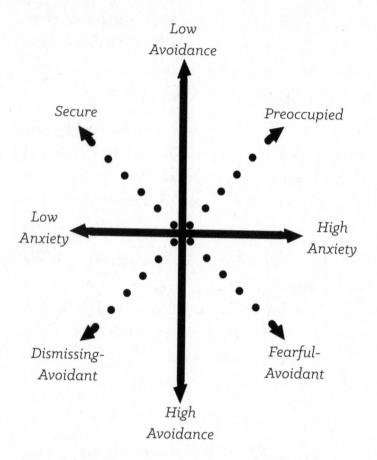

all over someone else's boundaries (and/or letting them stomp all over yours) in an effort to feel closer and more connected.

Which isn't to say you're fucked forever. Notice that I said a *moderate* correlation? This means that being mindful of your past and recognizing how it is informing the present can help you change your responses and rewire those reaction patterns. And we are gonna do just that later in the book.

Questions For Consideration

- How were your parents and other caretakers withdrawn or distant from you? What did they not know or understand about you? In what ways did they not support you or show up for you?

  - How did that affect your view of them and the world?

  - What rules about people did you develop based on these patterns?

- How were your parents and other caretakers entangled with you? How did they use you to meet their needs? What values, beliefs, and preferences did they have that they expected you to share).

  - How did that affect your view of them and the world?

- What rules about people did you develop based on these patterns?

- How have these worldviews and rules affected your current relationships?

- Do you notice any correlation between your attachment patterns and having boundaries that are too rigid?

- What about boundaries that are too permeable?

High-Conflict Personalities

When talking about boundary violations and where they go wonky, I would be feeding you a line of bullshit if I didn't discuss how certain types of personality traits are far more likely to lead to problems with relationship boundaries. Before I get to the worst of it, it's important to talk first about individuals who are high conflict. An individual with a *high conflict personality* (HCP) is someone with patterns of behavior that increase conflict rather than resolving it or reducing it in their life. It's not intentionally shitty, manipulative behavior...it's reactive, adaptive behavior.

I use HCP instead of terms that are clinical or diagnostic (like narcissistic or histrionic) because I'm not necessarily talking about mental illness and I don't want to pathologize how we are wired to respond to the world based on our past experiences. Getting into high-conflict mode is how many people try to feel back in control of a situation when they are feeling super out of control. And they often bust through other people's boundaries in the process.

And it's super common because being a human being isn't an easy task, is it? According to Billy Eddy, a therapist and lawyer who coined the term, about 15% of people in the US have high conflict personalities. For comparison, less than one percent of the population has been diagnosed with narcissistic personality disorder and less than two percent has histrionic personality disorder. I'd venture to guess most everyone, at some point in their life, has engaged in high conflict behavior. And some people (15% or so?) live in this space on the regular.

Oftentimes, people with more permeable boundaries have a bat-signal for high-conflict individuals because they will absorb enough crap from them that the HCP person doesn't have to examine their own shit or be held accountable for it.

The obvious question is who the fuck would want to fight with other people on the regular? Are HCPs just angry, shitty people? Not in the least, but their worldview sets them up to see conflict as a viable option for dispute resolution. If your past experiences have shown you that having your needs met is always a fight, then *you are always primed to fight.*

Let's look at some of the characteristics of a person with a high conflict personality, according to Eddy's High Conflict Institute:

Limited Emotional Self-Control: HCPs feel emotions very strongly and are almost entirely dominated by their negative emotions. Their responses often appear out of proportion to the event at hand. We are all hardwired to pay more attention to negative emotions because doing so is a survival instinct. We all have histories that inform our emotional responses to the world. Every one of us has had a response that seemed irrational to those around us but was absolutely our truth at the time. HCPs do so on the regular. It's not that they are wrong—they are just feeling what they are feeling, and not handling it well.

Limited Behavioral Self-Control: We are wired to react from our emotions, so if your emotions are coming in strong, your behavior is soon to follow if you don't have an awareness of what's going on. If you have limited behavioral self-control, your behaviors are very reactive and generally designed to control others so you can feel more in control.

Black and White Thinking: This typical thinking error refers to the brain's default setting of labeling things as good-or-bad, right-or-wrong, yes-or-no. And if something is perceived as bad or wrong, an HCP seeks to correct that. There may be a trillion other shades of grey options that are obvious to you, but they don't see the world in that way, so are blind to them.

Externalizing: HCPs see problems as external to them. They see that they are the ones who are being hurt, and not when they are the people doing the hurting. They do not take responsibility for their part in the interaction and blame others for their problems. It's an extreme reaction to the same fundamental attribution error that's wired into all of our brains. But remember that they are black and white thinkers, so if they see problems as coming from the outside, that means whoever they perceive as the problem is the person wholly responsible for its inception and resolution.

The point of this info isn't for you to go up to people in your life and say "According to Dr. Faith, you are obviously an HCP and you should stop your shit." The point is to help you better see the worldview of someone who appears to be operating from a place of continued combativeness. And to recognize that you may fall into this mindset, as well...at least in certain situations. The minute we start paying attention to our own bullshit is the minute it starts to change.

A lot of the communication tricks in the next section of this book are designed specifically for containing high conflict situations. Meaning, protecting your boundaries without setting off someone in a high-conflict mindset. And TBH, these skills work well in managing all kinds of different conversations in a boss way, even if dealing with someone who doesn't constantly have their fight-face on.

The first question is: Do you even need to respond?

When someone comes at you in a high-conflict way through text, email, or social media nastiness (and sometimes even when they do so in person) sometimes the best response is simply not to. Ask yourself:

1) What are the possible consequences of responding?

2) What are the possible consequences of not responding?

If I responded to every dumb, shitty thing people say, I wouldn't have any time left to write this book on how to respond to the dumb, shitty things people say. And it's amazing how quickly a lack of response can deescalate a situation. The more you practice this the more you will realize that not responding is often the better option.

However, sometimes not responding leads to other consequences, so you have to deal with that fuckitude. For example, if a colleague insists that a problem at work was your fault, you might need to respond or you could have consequences from your supervisor. If that's your current situation, it's totally cool to skip ahead (check out the BIFF communication skill in the chapter about communicating through conflict, later on in this book.)

But I have one last thing I really need to cover in this section of the book because it's far more common than we realize and needs to be talked about waywayway more than it actually is.

Coercive Control

I f all the other stuff we went into about how our boundaries got fucked up wasn't enough, there is one more huge area we need to address. A form of abuse that is almost always legal and involves the strategic application of boundary violations as a means of controlling another human being.

Coercive control refers to regular patterns of boundary violating behaviors that create fear-based compliance in someone. The term was coined by Evan Stark, whose 2007 book has the same name. His work brought to light how another person's systemic, organized boundary violations create an ongoing pattern of behavior that takes away our freedom of choice and ability to define our own personhood.

Dr. Stark's research shows that coercive control is present in up to 80% of abusive relationships. Which means only 20% of abusive relationships are defined purely by physical violence. Because it isn't something that is measured effectively (when it is measured at all), it is impossible to guess the number of relationships within the general population in which one partner abuses the other through these patterns of coercion.

Coercive control behaviors are not just a more extreme version of high conflict personality behaviors. High conflict responses are often the result of people perceiving their lives as out of control and they perceive conflict as their best means of regaining control. It *is* a boundary-busting behavior, and those of us who are more empathic can end up feeling attacked and manipulated by high conflict, but that's not the end goal of the person engaging in conflict.

Coercive control, by contrast, is strategic, rational, and ongoing...not reactive in the heat of the moment. Individuals who engage in coercive control are seeking the measurable material and social benefits they can achieve by shattering the psyche of another person in order to own them.

And because mind-games, degradation, isolation, intimidation, regulation, and an ever-changing "rule book" are not illegal actions, they are even more effective at holding another human being hostage than inflicting physical pain. It's not the physical abuse, it's the mind-fuck. It's emotional terrorism. And it's the real reason it's so hard to leave an abusive partner. And the reason that so many abuse survivors suffer from PTSD.

Once physical and sexual intimate partner violence started to become socially unacceptable in the 1970s, individuals who abuse had to find other ways to maintain control over their victims...the uptick in coercive control in the past few decades correlates strongly with an uptick in legal consequences for perpetrating physical and sexual harm on a partner.

Dr. Stark notes that coercive control is steeped in gender-based privilege (and in case you are wondering, he is a cis/het dude), therefore the focus of his work was on cisgender, heterosexual relationships in which men used coercive control techniques against their female partners. He notes that women are more vulnerable to coercive control because of their unequal political and economic status which allows cis men to systematically take advantage of us at greater levels. Which means we are again hitting how insidiously *normal* rape culture is.

The numbers in this regard don't lie, but in my experience as a therapist, I can absolutely attest to how coercive control extends beyond this narrow definition.. Coercive control exists within all manner of intimate relationships, in LGBTQ+ communities, among family members, within friendship groups, and within employer-employee relationships.

The common denominator of *unequal status* still applies to the dynamic of controller and controlled. Those with less power are far more susceptible to oppressive behavior by others whom they rely on for food, shelter, financial support, and/or safety.

How do these dynamics get created? It's a systematic, conscious process. Living in a society that centers power-over dynamics allows and even encourages means of owning the bodies and spirits of others. While most of us do not engage in that level of abusive power, there are plenty of people who do. There is a predisposition component (nature) to being a CC person, but it is far more a learned behavior (nurture). When people realize that they can perpetuate this kind of harm over another without consequence, they continue to do so.

A controlling individual sets the stage by cutting off their victim's means of support from the beginning. They seek out individuals who have vulnerabilities they can exploit. This may be people who are marginalized in significant ways (being poor, undocumented, isolated, etc.) or people who have the kind of abuse histories that have created permeable boundaries that the controlling individual can subvert almost immediately.

They set themselves up to become a rescuer in some fashion and create an indebtedness in their disempowered victim. They may rescue them financially from a bad situation. Or love bomb them with showered attention and care when they are at a low point and desperate for affection. They tether the vulnerable partner by ensuring more and more attachments to them and fewer attachments to others. At this point, resistance is worn down instead of strong-armed away.

Listed below are some of the more overt signs of being under the control of a coercive person, as well as some early-stage red flags to watch for. If you recognize yourself living these patterns, do know that there is support for getting out of an abusive situation. Even if they have never hurt you physically, domestic violence agencies can help you strategize a plan to leave safely (or stay safely, if that is your best option currently). See the back of this book for a list of resources.

Signs of a Coercively Controlling Person

When listed on paper, these activities seem pretty obvious, but when you are living this experience they sneak up in such a manner that we don't always see it until we step back.

The items on this list are based on the items used by researchers to measure coercive control in romantic partnerships:

- Controls/limits your contact with others (friends, family members, etc.) for instance by phone, internet, or chat.

- Wants all your passwords and access to all your accounts (but you don't have access to theirs)

- Tracks your movements through your cell phone (for your "safety")

- Makes demands regarding your movements (where you go, when you go, who you go with)

- Has physically stopped you from going somewhere or leaving the house (doesn't have to be by laying hands on you—they could block your exit, hide your keys, etc.)

- Spies on you/stalks you to check in on your movements

- Checks your clothes/receipts/items in the home for signs of your activities

- Audio or video tapes you either without your consent or by threatening you into consenting.

- Asks others about your activities (your children, family members, friends, neighbors)

- Makes demands about your appearance (that you look or dress a certain way for them, or maintain a certain weight)

- Controls household resources (bank accounts, vehicles, use of jointly produced income)

- Controls access to medical care

- Demands sexual intimacy in general, or specific sexual acts (either with them or with others on their demand)

- Controls use of contraceptives or STI prevention methods

- Interferes with or threatens your immigration/citizenship status

- Creates other legal trouble for you

- Threatens your housing stability (e.g., threatening to kick you out of a home they pay for, breaking rules set in a home rental to have your lease terminated and get you both evicted)

- Controls all parenting decisions and parenting tasks

- Threatens harm

- Displays physical violence towards others or property to frighten you (punching walls, hurting a family pet)

- Otherwise scares you into submission

- Threatens self-harm in retaliation for your behaviors

- Engages in self-harm in retaliation for your behaviors

- Keeps you from work/makes you late to work/ disrupts your workday/gets you fired

- Destroys your property

- Destroys the property of your friends and family

- Keeps weapons and makes threats (overt or veiled) to use them against you or someone else

Red Flags of a Manipulative Partner or Early Stage Coercively Controlling Partner

Along with the above, more overt behaviors, there are a lot of practices I see that also serve to wield power over another human being. These could be early warning sign behaviors in a new relationship that may become more intense as time goes on, or they could be occurring in longer-term relationships indicating a problem with systemic boundary violations. These behaviors are more belittling than controlling, but when done in a systematic way can invoke the process of wearing down resistance we see in coercively controlling relationships.

- Rude or dismissive of your friends and family

- Does not want you doing things with friends or family without their presence

- Excuses all their behavior rather than accepting accountability

- Needs constant contact with you through the day

- Engages in behaviors outside your value system and expects you to excuse them as "no big deal" or "jokes" (such as racial comments)

- "Jokes" about your appearance, passions, intelligence, culture, gender, or identity

- Challenges your worldview, motives, etc consistently (rather than asking to better understand them)

- Otherwise does not support your values and passions

- Picks fights so you feel obligated to make things up to them

- Always expects you to wait for their attention, doesn't value your time

- Never admits any fault in past relationships ending

- Expects you to be okay with their behavior when it's not okay for you to engage in same-said behavior

- Is rude to people they see as beneath them (service workers, waitstaff)

- Minimizes your feelings and dismisses how their choices and behaviors affect you in negative ways (such as accusing you of being too sensitive)

- Frames your disagreement as you not understanding or listening to them effectively

- Questions your judgement ("Oh, you're wearing that?")

- Challenges or belittles your decisions, even decisions with little consequence

- Threatens you with social embarrassment

- Disrupts the well-being of other people in your life in order to disrupt your well-being (your children, family members, loved ones)

- Makes you responsible for their happiness, stability, contentment

- Is jealous of attention you pay to others

Coercive Control Strategies Wielded toward Lesbian, Gay, Plurisexual, Trans, and Nonbinary Individuals

This list of power and control tactics is created by FORGE Forward, a website with a ton of great resources for trans people. I have found that many items on the list apply to relationships in which at least one person is not heterosexual, even if they are cisgender. Their list, with my additions based on my clinical experiences and the experiences of my friends, is below:

- Disregarding, diminishing, disrespecting your identity (names, pronouns, etc).

- Making fun or belittling these same identity markers

- Ridiculing your appearance

- Denying your identity (that you are not a real man, woman, enby, etc.)

- Using pejorative terms to describe you identity or aspects of your identity (including terms for body parts)

- Telling you no one will love you

- Telling you you are an embarrassment to communities to which you belong (LGBT community, church community, your bowling league, etc.)

- Refusing to let you discuss issues specific to your identity

- Threatening to out you to individuals you are not yet out to

- Weaponizing others' negative feelings about you to hurt you (e.g., having a fundamentalist preacher try to "save" you)

- Weaponizing the healthcare system or judicial system against you (threatening mental health commitments, police action, etc.)

- Restricting or denying access to medical affirmative care (therapy, hormones, surgery)

- Restricting or denying access to personal affirmative items (clothing, prosthetics, etc.)

- Fetishizing your body

Is Coercive Control a "Fixable" Thing?

Most people who set out to control others don't want to change; in these cases, it's much more important to focus on the safety of the victim. But that's not the case universally. Research demonstrates that when individuals experience therapeutic support that focuses on establishing equality and appropriate boundaries in relationships, along with behavioral strategies to manage violence and systematic desire to control, they can stop treating other people this way for good.

In fact, research shows that this type of support works better than incarceration for preventing future violence. Which makes total sense: the prison system is generally designed to perpetuate power-over models and reward power-over ways of thinking. The model developed by Ellen Pence in Minnesota, the *Domestic Abuse Intervention Project*, has demonstrated high success rates and is now used across the country.

There are also therapists who do this work in solo practice. You can search for offender treatment providers in your area, or call your rape crisis center and ask for clinician referrals.

And *yes*. I have worked with individuals who saw these red flags in themselves and wanted to unpack the histories that led them to this behavior, so they could make different and better choices in the future. And I have seen them go on to have healthy relationships. We can't go back and change our pasts, but we can make a conscious decision to say this behavior stops *here* and *now*, and make significant changes.

The big indicator of success in changing abusive behavior was that the coercively controlling individual had self-awareness of what they were doing and *wanted* to make that change. So if you see these red flags in your own behavior and are realizing that you *want* to change? That level of introspection is bad-ass. If this is work that you are looking to start in your own life, the last chapter in this book, and the *Unfuck Your Boundaries Workbook* accountability exercises, can be a good start...but you will likely need support in making some serious changes in your relationships. But having healthy, fear-free relationships in the future will be well worth the effort.

The No Test

Violence and abuse aren't overt in the beginning. They often start with a sense of ownership that moves into coercive control and, sometimes, external boundary violations. So even if you are in the throes of Something New (™) and things are pretty great, it's not a bad idea to see how New Person responds to boundaries.

The No Test is the brainchild of Australian domestic abuse counselor Rob Andrew, and it's amazingly simple. It is simply an evaluation of how someone responds to being told "no" for the first time.

It's far better to do this early on, and with smaller issues, before you're married and fighting over whether or not to baptize your kiddo.

Example: When Mr. Dr. Faith and I had been dating about a month, I had to attend a work holiday party. I mentioned going, and he said he would be happy to attend with me. When I responded with a *"No, thank you,"* he understood immediately and said, *"Too soon? I respect that."* Well played, Woke Bae.

You are looking for signs of control in their response. Someone being disappointed at being told no is totally normal. Someone being irritated or agitated at you not going along with their plan is a sign of a controlling personality. Do they argue the point? Do they try to force a "yes" rather than negotiate around your expectations?

The No Test can be an important part of the healing process for individuals who have been victims. It's about recognizing and prioritizing your boundaries over the comfort of others. Once you truly internalize your right to say no, you are far less likely to take responsibility for someone else's response to your boundary.

Stop! Grounding time: 5...4...3...2...1

Becauuuuuse. That was more rough stuff. So here's a chance to check in with yourself, make sure you're in the present and not super-activated. This grounding skill engages the five senses, which are the ways we connect to and stay present with the world around us. Give it a whirl. Or a count. Semantics.

1. Notice and name (in your out-loud voice or inside-your-brain voice) **five** things you **see** around you.

2. Now notice and name off **four** things around you that you can **touch.** You don't have to actually touch them, but you are totally welcome to.

3. Now notice and name off **three** things that you **hear.**

4. Now notice **two** things you can **smell.** It's totally kosher to go find something like the soap in the bathroom or something.

5. Now notice **one** thing you can **taste.** You can go find something to taste if you that's handy, but you can also just notice that you still taste your sandwich from lunch or your toothpaste from earlier in the morning. Whatever works.

Unfuck Your Boundaries

Now we are getting into the "fun" part of the book. I mean, relatively. No more discussions about the world being a dumpster fire. Just lots of information on being proactive in our day-to-day interactions. The skills in this part of the book will help us understand our own boundaries and communicate them even when it feels weird and uncomfortable to do so.

While we're at it, we'll learn how to evaluate the people around us and how we relate to them in terms of boundaries. We'll look at not just how well they respect ours, but how well we respect theirs—because we have all fucked that up at some point. And we'll talk about what to do when our boundaries are violated, and how to be accountable when we have violated the boundaries of other people.

We are creating cultural change here. Culture is everything we create, and we are engaging in the act of creation in a mindful, meaningful way. Remember when I said we are active participants in our own evolution? This is how we start.

Exploring Your Boundaries?

Understanding your own boundaries is the first step.

This is where we listen to, and within, ourselves and pay attention to the answers we find. While you do this part, it's totally okay if you have stuff bubble up that surprises the shit out of you. Or if you feel completely panicked because you have zero clue as to what your answer is. That's totally okay, friend. And utterly to be expected in a culture where we don't hear *"Hey, boundaries are a big thing, what's important to you?"* as we grow up.

Unless you're a cat (*"Touch one of my toe beans and I will end you"*), you probably have had some struggles in recognizing and communicating your boundaries. We work through our boundaries issues by paying attention to our gut reactions and longer-term responses to how people interact with us.

Explore your own boundaries in a conscious and mindful way. Ask people you trust to weigh in (your awesome friends, your rock star therapist, etc.) and see how your body resonates with what they say.

You are now at the point where you have a good idea of the area you most need to work in regards to your boundaries, whether it be stuff you are figuring out about yourself, stuff you need to work on communicating better with others (or at least certain others), etc. Here are some questions to start with. Grab a pen or paper (or your *Unfuck Your Boundaries Workbook*), or just give these some thought:

- What are some of your physical boundaries? Are they rigid, flexible, or permeable?

- Are there any issues you want to address regarding your physical boundaries? Anything you want to explore?

- What are some of your property boundaries? Are they rigid, flexible, or permeable?

- Are there any issues you want to address regarding your property boundaries? Anything you want to explore?

- What are some of your sexual boundaries? Are they rigid, flexible, or permeable?

- Are there any issues you want to address regarding your sexual boundaries? Anything you want to explore?

- What are some of your emotional-relational boundaries? Are they rigid, flexible, or permeable?

- Are there any issues you want to address regarding your emotional-relational boundaries? Anything you want to explore?

- What are some of your intellectual boundaries? Are they rigid, flexible, or permeable?

- Are there any issues you want to address regarding your intellectual boundaries? Anything you want to explore?

- What are some of your spiritual boundaries? Are they rigid, flexible, or permeable?

- Are there any issues you want to address regarding your spiritual boundaries? Anything you want to explore?

- What are some of your time boundaries? Are they rigid, flexible, or permeable?

- Are there any issues you want to address regarding your time boundaries? Anything you want to explore?

Now it's gut check time. Close your eyes, take a deep breath, and ask yourself these questions again.

- When you read all those questions above, what was your *emotional* response? Not what you *think* you should have answered, not what you know the intellectual answer to be, but what your *body* tells you the answer actually is.

- Did anything new come up?

- Was there anything that your body reminded you about that you had initially not listed?

If you're not sure what your gut reaction is or how to interpret it, the next exercise could help...doesn't that work out well?

A Loving-Kindness Boundaries Meditation

Loving-kindness (also known as Metta or Maitri meditation) is about honoring our desire to be free from suffering. It's a Buddhist concept—the more secular version is self-compassion. Self-compassion is the process of affecting positive change in our lives by being mindful of our experiences instead of being a total dick to ourselves for being fallible humans since doing so doesn't do anything to make us do better in the long run.

And boundary work is critical to self-compassion.

Self-compassion researchers Kristen Neff and Christopher Germer suggest that in order to find a loving-kindness mantra for yourself, you ask yourself:

What do I need? What do I truly need?

This process is a wonderful tool for figuring out your boundaries and holding them mindfully. This is typically done using the phrase "May I…" because Buddhist teachings use "may I" as a way of pointing the heart in a positive direction. Examples may include:

May I be free from unwanted touch

May I be respected for my beliefs

May I have space to think, feel, and dream

And it's okay if you have no fucking clue what you need. It really is. Realizing that you don't know something is the first step to figuring it out. After all, you were bopping along not even realizing that there was something there you weren't attending to, right? Maybe for you, the meditation is more like:

May I learn to tune into my authentic inner voice.

May I be compassionate to myself for struggling with this process.

May I be patient with myself as I discover what is important to me.

That's a weird little trick of the mind, isn't it? The idea that noticing that doing something is hard makes actually doing it a bit easier. Getting better isn't magical and instantaneous, but if you keep at it you will see results. Pinky swear.

Dealing with backdraft

Backdraft isn't just an early '90s movie starring Kurt Russell (although he's super cute in it), it's a real term used by firefighters. It describes what happens when the oxygen a fire has been feeding on has been used up and new oxygen enters the space, causing the fire to flare up again.

Neff and Germer, the self-compassion researchers talk about backdraft as a common part of the process of learning self-compassion. When we have shut ourselves off from our own needs for so long, paying attention to and communicating boundaries can become fresh oxygen igniting our old traumas, old attachment patterns, and old tapes about how we "should be." And then we feel like shit.

We may question our new attention to boundaries as the source of the negative feelings, rather than recognizing that the boundaries are the fresh oxygen. The old feelings are coming up so we can deal with them and release them (or, to follow the metaphor, let them die in the fire like they need to).

We may feel anxious. Or irritable. Or suddenly uncertain about things we felt pretty certain about. YMMV, so it's important to learn what backdraft feels like for you.

When discomfort arises, try the following:

1)   Label it for what it is, without beating yourself up. Use the same kindness you would use if you were talking to someone you love. "Oh, ok. That's

backdraft. That's really normal. In fact, that's a good sign that I'm doing difficult work."

2) Check in with yourself. Especially note your body sensations and your emotions and ask yourself "What do I need to feel safe right now so I can continue this good work instead of falling into old habits?"

3) Take any appropriate action steps toward relaying expectations about your boundary despite the discomfort you're experiencing.

4) If nothing pragmatic can be done, use a grounding skill or mindfulness skill (and what about that, I included one to try below!) to stay centered in your body until the feelings subside enough for you to feel back in control.

Measuring your breath by your footsteps

Find a place where you can walk relatively unencumbered. It doesn't have to be a straight path—walking in circles in your yard or around the parking lot of where you work is fine (and it worries people about your sanity so, bonus

Breathe normally. Meaning normal for you. Just however you breathe.

Cool. Walking and breathing. Got it?

Now figure out how many steps it takes for you to do an inhale and exhale cycle. There will be a rhythm to it. Everyone is a little different. Keep that shit up for a few more minutes. Walking and breathing...you are totally acing this whole therapeutic intervention thing like a boss. GETIT.

Okay. Now lengthen your out-breath by one extra step. Don't force it, let it ease into a longer outbreath naturally.

But you may notice a desire to lengthen your inhalation breath as well. If it feels good to do so, go ahead. Roll with this cycle for another 10 breaths.

Now lengthen the exhalation by one more footstep. Watch to see whether the inhalation also naturally lengthens by one step or not. Do the thing if your body is into it. Continue this pattern for 20 more breath cycles.

Now return to your normal breathing pattern. Are you still in the parking lot? Nobody has called for a mental health team to do a welfare check on you, have they? If you are still okay to keep walking, continue with your original (normal) breathing pattern for another 5 minutes.

If you are feeling it, move back to the lengthened breaths again, but for no more than 10 to 20 cycles before going back to your normal breathing (we don't want you getting lightheaded out there in the parking lot, after all).

Stop whenever you're ready. You're in charge of you.

How Do the People in Your Life Respond to Your Boundaries?

Boundaries are fundamentally relational. And not something we can really avoid since research shows our brains are hardwired for connection. Here's a place to gain some perspective regarding your boundaries-in-relation. Because we're looking for patterns here, right?

Take another look at those lists of boundary violations in the first part of the book. Read through them again and ask these important questions:

- Which people in your life respect the boundaries that you communicate? What do these people have in common?

- Which people do not? What do these people have in common?

If, generally speaking, most people in most situations don't respect your boundaries, then it's time to look at how you are communicating them. Maybe you aren't expressing them as effectively as you thought. This part of the book will help you work on that. So yaaay…help is on the way!

But if you are struggling more in specific relationships or with specific people who keep blowing past your boundaries, then you might, in fact, be dealing with an asshole, or an asshole-infused situation, like a really shitty office culture. Or systemic power-over injustice at a societal level, because let's not pretend that shit doesn't happen.

Before you apply some smackdown, and especially if you're looking at a newer relationship or situation, consider a few other possibilities for why your boundaries aren't being respected:

1. This person could have other stuff going on, such as medical or emotional health issues, that make attending to what you communicate difficult for them

2. This person might be autistic, making traditional conversation cues difficult for them to suss out

3. Maybe the individual is neurodiverse in other ways (eg, ADHD, traumatic brain injury) and has a hard time attending to relational, non-verbal signals and implicit messages

4. The person could have mental health issues that make them so internally focused that they don't have a real awareness of their impact on others

5. The person may feel so inferior to you that they don't see how their behavior impacts you

6. The person's behavioral compulsions could be so ingrained that they use violating the boundaries of others as a means of feeling more in control of the world

7. This person might be an abuse groomer digging in their heels in an attempt to get you under their emotional coercive control.

If the last scenario is the case, you know what you need to do: get out of there. Seriously, get yourself safe. If it's already escalated to violence, please get some support in making a safety plan. I'd start with the National Domestic Violence Hotline, which you can access by calling 1–800–799–7233 or logging into chat with someone at thehotline.org.

If the other scenarios are a possibility, it's time to have a different conversation. Ask the person how they respond and learn best and try adapting your communication style.

Chances are that with scenarios 1-3, you will need to take away any need for guesswork by expressing your expectations as concretely as pavement. Ask for their attention, express yourself clearly and directly, and elicit feedback regarding their understanding. For example:

> *Hey, friend person, I need to chat with you about something. I recently had a "well, duh" moment when I realized that I have a boundary that I haven't communicated with you. I'm not mad at you, it's totally on me to have told you. I know you're a hugger, and you hug me whenever we hang out together. And I love that about you. But I grew up in a family where I was forced to hug everyone, whether I was comfortable with it or not. Including some people who really creeped me out. Now I feel more comfortable when people ask if they can hug*

me before doing so. It's a body autonomy thing that's really important to me. I know that will make sense to you and you will respect that, so I feel comfortable telling you the whole story rather than making up some bullshit story about having a cold and not wanting to hug anyone. In the future, please ask me before you hug me and understand and respect that sometimes the answer will be no, but that has to do with me, not you. Does that make sense? Do you have any questions for me?

In scenarios, 4-6 you may find that responding to them as a high conflict person is the best course of action. Check out the section below on BIFF responses, it's a great tool for high-conflict conversations.

You may be in a situation where you just have to suck it up, too. I'm well aware. You have a shitty job you can't afford to leave. Or you have a shitty family that you can't, at this time, extract yourself from. You have to weigh your options before deciding to throw down over a boundary.

This is another place where the flexibility thing comes in. You will find that tolerating others' lack of respect for your boundaries *far* easier to manage when you acknowledge to yourself that you are making a choice to maintain the relationship rather than maintain the boundary. It may be the best choice for you at this moment. Remind yourself that this epic dickitude is just slightly better than the alternative, so you are choosing to accept it for right now. This perspective can really help you tolerate how upset and angry you feel. It may also propel you into creating the action plan you need to extract yourself from an increasingly shitty situation, rather than sitting in that slimepool of disrespect and disregard forever.

Questions for determining if a boundary is safely enforceable

- What kind of relationship do you have with this person (friend, family, co-worker, rando at the co-op, etc.)?

- Are y'all on the same level or does one of you have power over the other (is someone the boss, has societal privilege, a parent that pays the bills, etc.)?

- Is this relationship time-limited (are you stuck with having to deal with this mofo on the regular)?

- What would you like to tell this person if you could say everything without any consequence?

- What are the consequences if you say those things?

- Are the consequences manageable? Is there a way to make them more manageable?

Communicating Your Boundaries and Consent

Communication is *how we do* boundaries and consent. I know I've been guilty of nurturing a world of butthurt that would have been easily prevented if I had just used my words. Unless you are a total specimen of perfection, you've probably done the same at some point. Changing how we engage can make all the difference in the world.

There's a linguistics theory called the Sapir-Whorf hypothesis that talks about how what we think informs how we speak (and we all get that part) and *also* how the way we speak starts to change how we think. Someone exposed to racist language, who starts taking on some of those linguistic tendencies, will eventually code themselves into overtly racist actions.

The brain is just a huge sponge when it comes down to it. So understanding our language patterns and making active changes in them will create better ways to negotiate the world, and better ways to recognize, uphold, and communicate boundaries.

Communication Styles

First, let's look at styles of language patterns and how they relate to our boundary styles. These are all the ways you might find yourself communicating in different situations and with different people.

Aggressive communication style tends to be excessively harsh. This is the general go-to for people who have rigid boundaries. Aggressive communicators tend to interrupt others, disregard others' opinions, and continually reinforce their own worldview and "rightness." Have you ever met anyone like this? Seen a politician on TV act like this? You know the type. If you admit you are waiting for pumpkin spice latte season to start, they roll their eyes and tell you that's bougie and dumb, your taste is shitty, and you need to stop. *The meta-message of aggressive communicators is "I'm cool and you're a dumbass."*

Passive communication style tends to be ineffective in helping people protect themselves and hold their center, so it makes sense that this is the communicating strategy for people with permeable boundaries. Passive communicators often don't make their wants and needs known, and say that things are fine when they are really, totally, deeply not fine. Passive communicators tend to defer to others, praising them while dumping on themselves. This isn't the same thing as letting someone you know and trust help guide you to better decision-making in a crisis. This is about never feeling like you can authentically advocate for what is right for you. Passive communicators might say "Oh, pumpkin spice lattes! Let's get those. I mean, I'm lactose intolerant and I'm gonna get really sick, but I can deal. It's totally okay." *The meta-message of passive communicators is "I'm a hot mess, but you're totally cool, so you make the decisions for both of us."*

Assertive communication style is our sweet spot in most cases (unless your literal safety is on the line and being situationally aggressive or passive makes sense) and is the general hallmark of people with flexible boundaries. Assertive communicators are firm in their belief systems and speak in a way that is congruent with their actions but still respects differing viewpoints. Back to the PSL example I apparently cannot let go of: if you say you want your pumpkin spice latte, they may respond with "Glad to see you out there living your best life, loving what you love. Could you order me an iced americano, though? That's more my jam." *The meta-message of assertive communicators is "I'm cool and you're totally cool, too. Even if we don't agree."*

Some questions to reflect on:

- What is your communication style most of the time? Is it different in different circumstances or with different people?

- What messages have you internalized about your right to healthy communication and ownership of your values and beliefs?

- If you communicate differently in certain situations, or with certain people, what about those relationships causes you to change?

- How close is your current communication style to what your ideal balance would be?

- What is the first place you can start to shift your communication style, moving closer to your ideal? How will you go about doing that?

If you don't communicate as well as you would like to, owning that is really important.

As in, *"Hey friend! I realized recently that I don't communicate things that are important to me nearly as well as I should. Like the other night when I agreed to meet you for coffee but then didn't drink mine and complained the whole time and you ended up confused AF, which is understandable. I'm working on that. So what I've been trying to say, albeit, not well, is, next time we hang out can we go for a walk instead? Or something else without the temptation of delicious coffee drinks that make me sick but I still can't resist them?"*

If you have this conversation, I'm totally awarding you a gold star for badass adulting.

The biggest thing to remember here that it is a process. You may need to ask each other questions and keep figuring things out. You may have to clarify what you mean until it comes out right. The person you have had communication struggles with may resist the entire conversation (which means you have an entirely different issue). This ain't easy shit.

I Statements

Learning to communicate your boundaries more assertively and effectively doesn't require a weekend Tony Robbins retreat. It just means considering effective communication as a skill, learning that skill, and practicing until it becomes second nature.

Try this when communicating to someone else when you are all kinds of hacked off (or all kinds of thrilled, for that matter):

I feel ————————————————————

when you ————————————————————

What I want is ——————————————

You know what this is? Being a grown-ass person who takes responsibility for their own feelings and actions and clearly communicates their needs, rather than blaming other people ("You made me mad!") or doing the freeze-out-no-talking thing ("If you really knew me you would know this was important right now!").

It's gonna feel all kinds of weird and awkward at first. I've had lots of people tell me that they bust out laughing the first few times they try it. It's just so *unnatural*, isn't it? Because we don't encourage people to talk like this, taking accountability and responsibility for their feelings.

But we *should*.

Our feelings are completely our own, and we shouldn't blame others for them. We can, however, ask them for different behaviors that better respect our boundaries. This skill works in regular communication and stays in place even if your convo has leveled up to conflict level. Staying with ownership of your own feelings completely shifts away from the blame game.

You can even take an extra step in acknowledging that they didn't intend the distress you felt, for instance, by adding:

I felt uncomfortable when you made that joke just now. I know you just meant it to be funny and thought I would laugh rather than be upset. But I struggle with jokes about that topic. I would really appreciate it if you didn't tell jokes like that around me.

That's awesome shit right there. And bonus points on this, because other people can't tell you how to feel if you are taking ownership of it. It's not right or wrong, it's just what you feel. Adulting FTW.

The Four Levels of Communication

We are all trying to communicate better. Boundaries are expressed in dialogue right? When you think about it, boundary negotiation is a huge fucking percentage of our communication with others. Communicating with the "I statements" model is a great strategy for being more mindful of that process. But figuring out where the breakdowns come from the most often is also hugely beneficial. I first heard this model in an online course I was streaming on Neuro-Linguistic Programming. I can't find a reference to it anywhere, so I don't know the origin story (and if you do, please drop me a line). Discussing an idea without the appropriate citation and attribution upsets my little academic heart, but it's too brilliant to not share.

The basic idea is that each exchange of verbal dialogue has four levels:

1) *What we mean to say*. You know, the actual idea you are trying to express.

2) *What we actually say.* If you are really good at saying only exactly what you mean at all times, I hope you write a book on your technique. For us regular humans, what we have in our minds and what comes out of our mouths is not always a solid match.

3) *What the other person hears.* Just because you said it doesn't mean they heard it without any filter.

4) *What the other person thinks you mean.* Even if you said "anything for dinner is fine" and you *meant* anything for dinner is fine, your partner may think there is a hidden agenda, or other things going on beyond the words that actually came out of your mouth.

Everyone I have worked with who is struggling with a communication breakdown (with a partner, with family, with coworkers) has a problem in at least one of these areas. Generally, we are high achievers and are activating more than one if not all of them. Figuring out where the breakdown is informs the strategies to repair it.

Let's say you are assigned a group project (fucking hell like no other) and your group is figuring out the task assignments.

1) *What you mean to say.* Maybe growing up, you weren't allowed to voice much opinion. Maybe you tend to think your answers are wrong. Maybe you get up in your head about what you want and get paralyzed when trying to communicate. If you don't express yourself well (or aren't great at figuring out what you want), being more measured and considered before speaking or responding can make a huge difference. Maybe you want to put together the big work presentation but not do the talking part. This is what you intend to get across to the rest of the group, right?

2) *What you actually say.* Here is where you gotta use your words. This is easier said than done for a lot of folks. Say you shrug and say *"I'll do the powerpoint or whatever."* This doesn't translate well to *"Please for the love of everything holy don't make me do the public speaking part."*

3) *What the other person hears.* We all have our own interpretations, filters, and distractions. For this example, let's say you communicate pretty clearly *"I get the fear-sweats like whoa if I have to speak in front of other people, I want to stay behind the scenes and put together the ppt instead."* And someone in the

group only hears part of that and writes down that you are going to do the ppt, and do the introduction of the project and the main speaker. This happens sooooo often, unfortunately. It goes back to being lossy, we don't listen well, we get distracted, etc, etc. If this is someone you communicate with on the regular, it's helpful to have them repeat back in their words what you just told them. As in, "I heard you say…" In this kind of situation, you may respond with *"The fear-sweats are real, I don't want to speak for the group at all, even the intro. Calling EMS when I pass out won't speak well to the project."*

4) *What the listener thinks you mean.* So many people have had past interactions where all responses were a death trap, they were supposed to mind read and interpret everything that was told to them, and there was hell to pay if they didn't. A lot of people will over-interpret what you say, they may benefit from a reminder that *you* are responsible for your responses, and they don't have to mind-read. If you say "I don't mind any assignment on the project" and they are worried that they are supposed to figure out your preference, you can remind them that you are responsible for how you communicate and you

genuinely meant that you had no preference. If you catch yourself overinterpreting, here's your chance to remember that you are not a mind reader, and people are responsible for what they say to you.

By paying attention to our weak spots in communication exchanges, and actively working to strengthen them we are *automatically* going to be better at expressing and respecting boundaries. It's an automatic adulting level-up.

Communicating What We Do Want Instead of What We Don't Want

Cristien Storm's book *Empowered Boundaries* makes the point that while there is nothing inherently bad about a hard "no" regarding what we don't want, communicating what we do want opens up whole other avenues for dialogue and negotiation. A simple example?

Person 1: How about sushi for dinner?

Person 2, Option 1: Ugh, no.

Person 2, Option 2: I'm really in the mood for a hamburger. I'd like to go there if you are interested? Or we could grab takeout from both places and then we can both get exactly what we are feenin' for.

The second option opens up a completely different conversation and negotiation options.

But not all "what we want" communications are sushi and hamburgers. Sometimes it requires a level of vulnerability that is really hard to articulate. This means that more than just adhering to a boundary we have to authentically identify our desires and communicate them more effectively, right?

Example:

Person 1: How about I gag you and tie you up when we have sex tonight?

Person 2, Option 1: Absolutely not.

Person 2, Option 2: What I would really like to explore is prostate stimulation. How do you feel about using a toy on me designed for that?

See how the second option carries far more risk for the asker? I get into more detail regarding these kinds of interactions in my consent zine, using Betty Martin's wheel of consent, but this serves to illustrate how sometimes while a full-stop no is a perfectly acceptable answer, an expression what you DO want can create huge shifts in understanding yourself and communicating that more effectively with the people in your life.

Question: Who would be a safe person in your life for you to experiment on communicating your boundary about what you do want instead of what you don't want?

Communicating through Conflict and Disagreement

Most of the communication tools in this chapter work in power-with situations where everyone in the conversation has each others' best interests at heart. But there are tons of situations in life where there's a conflict, be it about where to get coffee or how to regulate nukes, and there isn't existing trust in the relationship or maybe you're dealing with a high conflict person, someone who is freaking out, or someone who truly doesn't care if there's a mutually beneficial resolution.

A powerful tool for these situations is the BIFF Response—Brief, Informative, Friendly, and Firm—paired with avoiding the 3 As—Advice, Admonishment, and Apologies. These are tools from Bill Eddy's High Conflict

Institute and I teach them to people on the regular. They are great tools for handling conflict and also with situations that are emotionally charged in general.

If you are in the process of establishing and holding better boundaries with someone for the first time, it's going to feel emotionally charged since it's all weird and awkward and new for everyone involved. Having a bit of a recipe will help a ton. Try this one. Add extra garlic if you're feeling sassy.

Brief: Don't give any extra info. Don't over-explain. The more you write or say, the more fodder you are giving the aggrieved party for their battle, yeah? Let's say you got an angry missive from your boss, accusing you of jacking the keys to the dumpster. Instead of writing an eight-paragraph defense, try a brief, factual response: "I clocked out two hours before closing last Thursday, so I didn't carry out the garbage that day and I never used the keys."

Informative: Don't focus on their incorrect statements, focus on your accurate ones. No sarcasm, no negging, no remarks about the other person's personality, ethical choices, etc. We are looking to end the conflict, not throw down about who the real dumbass in this scenario is. In the same work example, you might add the information, "In order to refresh my memory, I double checked the calendar. I wasn't the person who closed that day, it was Xander."

Friendly: I know, it doesn't seem fair that you have to be nice when someone else is showing their ass. The best way of coming out of the conflict unscathed is to not match hostility with hostility. This doesn't mean fake nicey-nice...just civil. You are far more likely to get a neutral response, if not a positive one. Going back to the work example, you could phrase it as something like "Hi, Sarah! Xander and I did both work last Thursday, but I clocked out early because it was so slow and Xander closed by themself, so I don't know where the keys to the dumpster ended up."

Firm: Be firm without being threatening. Don't make comments that can invite more discussion (e.g., "Let me know if you have any questions" or "I hope you agree that..."). Back to Xander the key-stealer? You could close with "I wish I could be of more help, hopefully Xander will be." Think like Forrest

Gump. As in "that's all I have to say about that." If you need to get a decision from someone and can't end the discussion here, another feature of "firm" is offering two choices so you don't have continued over-discussion.

If you get more communication after you have already BIFFed your response, you can either ignore it or broken-record your BIFF response with the same keywords and even less content until they give up.

Another Bill Eddy trick for BIFF communication is to avoid the three A's: Advice, Admonishments, and Apologies. So let's look at those, as well:

Advice: You don't want to give anyone advice on how to manage themselves or the situation they are ramped up about. They are already hot under the collar so you won't get anywhere. I know I don't hear much when I'm butthurt—that's a pretty universal response. Notice that rather than telling Sarah to check the timecards in my example, I said "I double checked the calendar and confirmed…" That avoided giving her advice on how to do her job. She will realize she should have done so herself once she calms down, so it's all good.

Admonishments: You may want to offer corrective feedback, but just like advice-giving, this isn't the time. The point of a BIFF response is to defuse an emotional conversation and end it for the time being. So avoid anything that makes it sound like you are explaining their behavior to them like they are a naughty child. Again, with Sarah the manager, imagine the continued battle if you had said, "If you had acted like an actual manager, you would have checked the schedule before having a ragefit at me"???

Apologies: Authentic apologies are a good thing. But when everyone is activated is not the time for them. Apologizing can give the other person something to blame us for, extending the conversation. "I'm so sorry I don't know what happened to the keys" can let Sarah continue to blame you for her ridiculous insistence that you are somehow responsible. A more gentle "social apology" *can* be helpful to diffuse the issue, if you want to add that to the mix, however. "I'm so sorry you are having to deal with such a frustrating situation with everything else on your plate!" is a show of commiseration and empathy that doesn't connect you to the blame game and doesn't give Sarah any more ammo.

Keeping Your Cool When Communication Fails

I know, I know what you are thinking. No matter how boss you are at BIFFing your communication there are some motherfuckers who aren't gonna hear shit from you. Even if you added interpretive dance to the mix, they are so wrapped up in their bullshit they are determined to hear everything you say through that world view. And in those times when absolutely nothing you do or say will lead to effective communication.

Sometimes you can't stand your ground, even politely using BIFF statements for a multitude of reasons. Maybe they are family members on whom you are financially dependent. Maybe it's a shitty boss at a shitty job that you can't afford to quit. No matter what your circumstances, I am well aware that if "just walk away" were really that simple, everyone would do it.

These two skills focus less on communication and more on how to protect yourself from someone else's onslaught...which is sometimes the only way we can set a boundary.

The pane of glass trick

Are you stuck with motherfuckers who push every last button? One of the tricks I've found that has really helped me is to imagine a clear pane of glass between me and them. I can hear and see them, but their emotional bullshit stops at the glass.

This is especially helpful for us Counselor Troi empath-type people. We can respond to the content of their words and actions without being emotionally drained by whatever forces are driving them.

And for those of us whose empathy leads us into doing more for others than we should (like rescuing, excusing, or caretaking that isn't healthy in the long run for anyone involved) it can help us remain proactive instead of reactive in a difficult relationship dynamic.

The grey rock method

Another trick for dealing with boundary-busting individuals or just toxic, shitty situations in which someone is being harmful, is the grey rock method.

A blogger who goes by Skylar on the 18orule.com developed what she calls the "Gray Rock Method" as a tool for convincing abusive individuals to leave *you*, by making yourself as boring and non-responsive as possible. You essentially become a grey rock. The more boring you are, the less fuel they have. You are essentially training them to consider you an unsatisfying conquest.

This is a tool that I had unconsciously put into practice as a teen and can testify to how well it works. I had a grandparent who commented frequently on my weight and body shape. I remember him picking up my arm when I was about 14 and declaring, *"You ain't got no wrists!"*

My response? *"Mmmmm, ok."*

The conversation ended right there, due to my complete lack of reaction.

One of my interns does on-call work for a local hospital that tends to be perpetually short-staffed and operating in chaos. Her supervisor was blowing up her phone, wanting to pick up shifts outside her availability. I coached her through a BIFF response, but her supervisor continued to rant...trying to guilt my intern with comments like *"I don't have any to cover! I don't know what to do! I really need help!"*

My intern responded with *"Yeah that's a lot"* and then stop responding. Eventually the rant ceased...and the haranguement was never made mention of again. If my intern had continued defending herself, her responses would have been used to as proof that being short staffed was *her* fault, not the supervisor's.

When Do You Need to Justify Your Boundaries?

Now that we have gone on and on and on about the different types of boundaries, the range of ways we enforce them, and THEN how to communicate them (holy shit...I think we all earned a graduate degree in boundary-setting at this point, what do you think?), let's talk about the complicated terrain of when and how we justify our boundaries to others (I think this means we are now getting into a PhD boundaries class, don't you?). I've found in my private practice that the one thing that feels worse than setting boundaries, is the need to legitimize them once we set them. If your boundaries have been really permeable in the past, it's easy to fall into the trap of over-explaining as you firm them up, even in situations that are not high conflict.

In her book *Empowered Boundaries*, Cristien Storm explains how we sometimes get hooked into feeling a need to defend or justify our boundaries. You know, the relational labor we put into the overexplain of our boundary that is generally not nearly as necessary as we think it is.

When I read that my first thought was of Pema Chodron's definition of *shenpa*. The Tibetan word is usually translated as "attachment" but I prefer Chodron's translation, which means "hooked." It's that feeling of going down a well-worn path or getting caught in a record scratch that creates a continuous skip. Chodron describes it as that feeling of being trapped in a situation that doesn't feel good, causing us to tighten up and shut down.

Boundary work can trigger shenpa just like any other situation. The hook, in this case, is feeling the need to justify a boundary we are setting. Or convince someone else to understand our boundary. Advocating for ourselves can feel really uncomfortable, and a lot of people get an urge to justify their self-advocacy.

Boundary shenpa is the result. Being in our feels about setting or holding a new boundary is so uncomfortable, we go into our headspace instead. And start intellectualizing the whole process to ourselves and the person with whom we are setting the boundary. This prevents us from being authentic with ourselves and with others.

Justifying a boundary isn't always a bad thing. It depends on the situation, right? If a friend asks if I can attend her event, I can say "no" as a complete response. Or I can say "I'm sorry, I'm actually in the office that day…I'll be exhausted afterward and will really need to go home and rest." Some justifications are relationally relevant, which is not the same thing as boundary shenpa.

Boundary shenpa occurs when "No, I'm not comfortable with you borrowing my car" turns into an over-explanation, or even falsehoods, to justify your no. "I'd totally let you use my car, but I have errands to run/the brakes are spongy/etc, etc." Because we don't feel comfortable with our own boundary and don't want to upset the other person or have them think we're being shitty, so we get into justification mode.

What's the antidote to boundary shenpa? The Tibetan word here is *shenlock*. It refers to a renunciation of an old pattern. When you notice that physical response of tightening into a need to over-justify, try to recognize the habit in yourself with loving-kindness, and respond with the new boundary-setting habit we are working to become more natural. Practice how you are going to set your boundaries and how you are going to respond if someone *does* get butthurt. Some ideas:

- *"No, I'm not comfortable with you borrowing my car."*

- *"I see that you are upset by my answer, and I respect that but I'm not going to lend you my car."*

- *"Be that as it may, my answer is no."*

Recognizing these patterns and changing our interactions isn't of those things where we have a huge breakthrough, make a seismic change, and then never have a problem again. It took years and years to develop our ways of communicating, and it will take a while to learn to do it differently. And all of this is like the train of dominoes, where they are laid in a row, and knocked down in a particular order. Old communication patterns that no longer serve us are some of the first dominoes we target.

How Do You Respect Other People's Boundaries?

O k, so now that we have a better idea of your own boundaries... That was a fuck-ton of emotional work, wasn't it? Ugh, yeah. Let's go ahead and finish off the navel-gazing by looking at how you respond to the boundaries of others.

1. Generally speaking, do people tend to respond positively to you? Do they tell you they feel comfortable sharing with you? That you hear them without judgment?

2. Do you have people (or at least one person) in your life with whom you are able to have deep and authentic exchanges of ideas and feelings?

3. Are you able to maintain these relationships over a long period of time?

4. What kinds of situations make it hard for you to respect the boundaries of others? Is it with certain people? Or when people are making certain decisions that cause you concern?

The first three questions are a good self-examination of whether or not you are able to maintain relationships. If you struggle with the boundaries of others, it will start to eat away at all of your interpersonal relationships. Let's be honest. Do you know anyone who is bad at boundaries but somehow still maintains healthy relationships? I don't.

If you read the first three questions and had an "Oh, *fuck*" moment, that doesn't mean you should put down the book and immediately start emotionally self-flagellating, okay? We generally learn good or bad boundary setting from those around us. If no one modeled healthy boundaries for you in the past, how were you supposed to learn? And since no one is handed the boundaries manual at birth, a lot of us have to figure it out later. As you start being mindful of boundaries in your interactions, I bet you will see serious, positive changes in your relationships overall.

The fourth question is more universal. Because I *promise* we all have situations where we struggle to respect other people's boundaries. It might be with family members you care about, when you see a friend making the same dumb decision for the 97th time, or when someone engages in a behavior that you've previously seen lead to a bad end for yourself or others. Those kinds of situations can really make it hard to respect their boundaries.

And it's okay to communicate that. To say something in the vein of:

I'm having a hard time respecting your boundaries right now because I'm really worried about you. I don't want to start bossing you into doing what I want you to do. It might be better if we don't discuss this particular issue because I can't really be impartial.

It's the nicest way I can think of it to avoid a *"Your new bae is a piece of shit! Break up with them!"* conversation that's only going to get you into trouble.

It's also okay to ask for clarification on what level of support someone is looking for. I struggle with the boundaries of my adult kiddos. Makes total sense, right? I still want to parent them. When they ask for my advice, I ask straight out: *Do you want the mom answer or the supportive-adult-in-your-life answer?* This gives them the opportunity to let me know how flexible their boundaries are about my interference in the situation, and has probably saved us from any number of fights over the years.

Handling No

Nobody likes to be told "no." Being told no sucks. It makes our inner toddler kick and scream, and all those toxic societal messages start to leak out in response. But the word "no" (or other words and actions that convey it) is one of the most important ways people express boundaries. What if we started paying attention to "no" messages in a conscious way, and dealt with being told no like bad-ass adults? These are some of the strategies that help:

1) **Pay attention to your feelings with self-compassion.** If we stuff our feelings, they are just gonna explode out later, like an overstuffed garbage bag. It's ok to think "ow, that hurt...I was really wanting that to happen"

2) **Put "no" in its proper place.** No is generally the rejection of your offer, not your personhood. Quite rarely is someone saying that everything about you is wrong and unwanted and fundamentally broken. Our inner demons may tell us that when

someone doesn't want to hang out with us, but it's bullshit. There are tons of good humans in the world that I don't want to work with, go to parties with, or see naked. I know you feel the same way... and it's important to remember that others can feel that way about you without it being symbolic of something greater.

3) **Recognize the boundary you hit and learn from it**. If someone tells you no, they are setting a boundary. This is good information about them and your relationship with them. This is the whole point of this book, isn't it? To recognize and communicate and respect boundaries? "No" is the space where we start seeing where the boundaries are erected.

4) **Communicate this understanding.** Don't wheedle or try to convince. Don't pout around slathered in butthurt. Say *"I'm bummed, but I get it, no hard feelings."*

Respecting people's boundaries is how we make our relationships ·better. People will know they can trust you with their truth and that you will respect them and understand that they aren't attacking your personhood. It makes you *the embodiment of safe space*. And it also serves to reinforce that if we can do that work for others than we deserve the same work done for us. Win-win.

S.T.F.U.

I have a confession to make. I get super excited about shit and tend to verbally run over people. Especially when I'm being quiet and listen-y at my clinic all day, I get way too jabbery after hours. An ex of mine called me "Mistress Interuptess" which was a nice (and funny) way of pointing out when I was on my bullshit in that regard.

Because I wasn't *communicating* effectively if I wasn't *listening* effectively. And I was definitely going to end up unintentionally hulk-smashing people's boundaries if I was being oblivious to what they were saying.

I love Sarah Mirk's book *Sex From Scratch: Making Your Own Relationship Rules*. I was skimming through my well-worn copy recently and found a hot-pink highlighted paragraph that really resonates with the ideas I am endeavoring to share here.

Sarah shares a communicating strategy she learned from a tech entrepreneur named Matthew. While *shutting the fuck up* is something that most of us need to do at some point, his acronym is a little different and is wonderful advice for all kinds of communication. And it will improve your boundary identification game by like 33 ½ percent. I made that stat up just now, but it WILL help. If you are listening differently, you are HEARING differently.

S.T.F.U stands for:

Share Time: Conversation is a two way street. Being silent and listening is just as important a role as talking. My bad-ass editrix actually saw Matthew's talk on this technique and tells me that he offered a math equation to help people conceptualize how to share time in a simple way. He suggests dividing the amount of time you have for the interaction (say an hour) by the number of the people in the room (say six) and make sure you don't spend more than your portion of the time talking (in this case, ten minutes).

Three Seconds: Give others a chance to continue to speak or jump into the conversation before you begin to speak. That means counting to three when there is a pause in the conversation before making your own verbal contribution.

Find Empathy: Really listen to people...not just the content but their backstory. Where are they coming from?

Understanding Is Not Necessary: I really love this one. Active listening is designed to help us better understand others, right? But that doesn't mean we always are successful at doing so. We've all had a what-the-literal-fuck moment in regard to someone else's worldview. It's okay to simply accept it as theirs without "getting" it. And maybe further marination on what they are saying will give you an aha moment later?

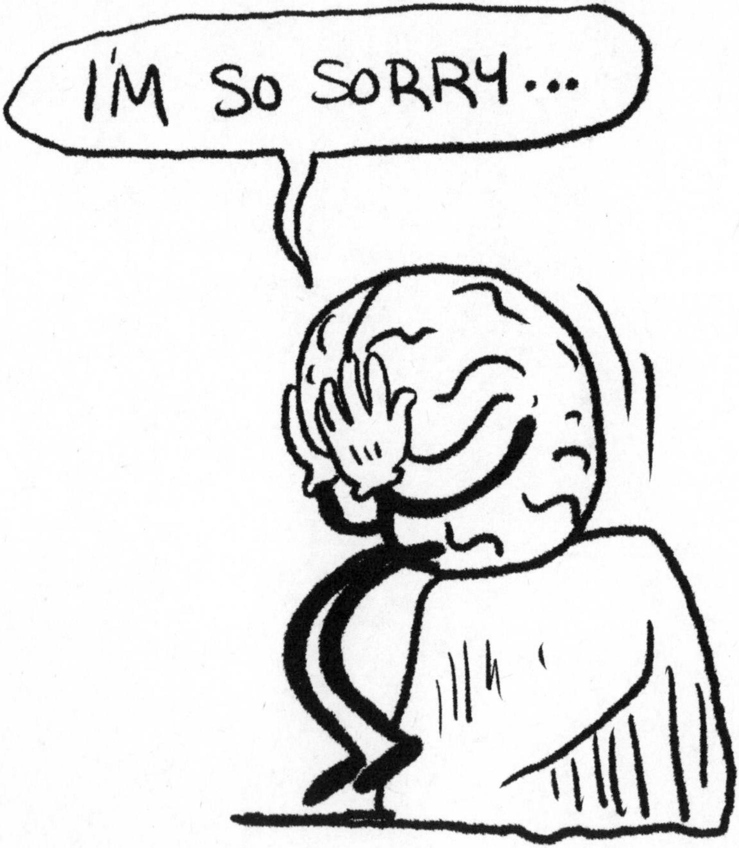
I'M SO SORRY...

Holding Yourself Accountable for Boundary Violations

We've all had boundaries violated by others *and* done some boundary violating ourselves.

This can range from horrific actions like the rape and abuse we discussed earlier in this book to the more everyday crappy things we do like finishing off the last of the ice cream even though you knew your roommate was saving it for later. There are always places where we could have done so much better in terms of autonomy and respecting others.

Being an adult means examining the messages we've received our entire lives critically so we can make better and more informed choices for ourselves and the world around us. Recognizing we are the product of our experiences helps us unpack the messages we received in the past, either from family, friends, or greater culture. Part of this process includes dealing with the consequences of having violated others' boundaries. I've had a lot of people tell me that they carry deep guilt for past actions.

Guilt is not a signal that you are an irredeemable shithead, it's a signal that you have work to do. That you now *know better* and are committing to *doing better*. And that essential work happens through the process of accountability.

Accountability is the willingness or self-propelled obligation to accept responsibility for and repair the harm caused by our actions. It may mean listening to and holding space without defensiveness for another person's experience of how your actions have caused them harm (which is wayyyyyyy harder than most people think) so you can offer an apology and interact differently in the future.

It may mean doing some big soul-searching, self-examination type work about how you have walked in the world for many years. Individuals who have engaged in substance use find this to be an important part of their recovery. But they aren't the only ones. Those of us who had significant trauma histories will often continue those cycles of abuse and pain, systematically hurting others and themselves the way they have been hurt. Unpacking generations of toxic, reactive behavior takes a huge amount of work. But that work is how we heal ourselves, those around us, and future generations. You've heard the expression "hurt people hurt people and healed people heal people?" Cheesy with extra cheese, I know. But so so true. We can't change the past but we CAN say "this is where the harm stops."

Accountability work is difficult. But it's essential to having healthy relationships despite the boundary violations that we inevitably do to each other. As brain science bears out, we are a species that is hardwired for relationships. That means we need relationships to survive, but it doesn't mean we always do a good job at them. Accountability *should* feature prominently in our relationships, personal lives, and professional lives.

Reflect on one of the moments I know you've been thinking about where you violated someone else's boundaries. Are you still in contact with them? Do you have the sort of relationship where you could have a discussion about what happened and either request or give an apology? As in *"Remember that time I ate your ice cream? I was thinking about it and I really owe you a sincere apology. You were saving it for when you had a hard day, and then your day sucked even more when it wasn't there. I can't go back in time but I can do and be better in the future."* Notice that this apology didn't include any explanation about *why* you ate the ice cream or blame for the other person not eating it sooner. It's about healing your relationship, not excusing yourself.

Or if you're asking for accountability from someone else, you might say, *"Remember last month when we went out for drinks and I said I didn't want to have more than two beers but you ordered a few rounds of shots and said 'don't worry about it, we're walking home so it's no big deal if you drink them'? I was really uncomfortable with what. I felt pressured to drink more and was frustrated that you weren't respecting my earlier request. I ended up drinking them, then was obviously mad at you about it. We can't go back in time but I can be better at expressing my boundaries so you can be clearer on respecting them."*

Also? This is a personal soapbox of mine, fair warning. You need to apologize without justifying your behavior. For instance, "I'm sorry—I didn't have any money for lunch so I took yours from the fridge," is the opposite of an apology. It's a justification. It's doubling down against their hurt feelings.

Defensiveness about unintended consequences is also unhelpful. "I ran your car into the light pole but I didn't mean to" is frustratingly unhelpful, even if you add a "sorry" somewhere in the mix. Nobody assumes that intentionally running a borrowed car into a light pole was on your agenda. Instead, try, *"I'm so sorry I ran your car into the light pole. It's my responsibility to have it fixed."* This apology includes *language of accountability*, which means owning the consequences of our actions, honestly and completely.

This is a real, completely true story of a conversation I had with my late husband. He came in from the backyard and announced that my chiminea (which is a clay fire pot if you are wondering) was broken. When I asked what happened, he said *"It dropped. And it broke."* When I asked where it dropped from he said *"Well, I was moving it. And it fell out of my hands. So it broke when it dropped from my hands."*

(I know in reading this it seems like a ridiculous explanation but people explain their actions like this ALL THE TIME once you start paying attention.)

We must have gone round and round for another ten minutes of me saying *"So you dropped my chiminea and broke it?"* and him arguing *"NO! It dropped and broke!"*

When he finally said *"Yes! Fine! I dropped it and broke it but I didn't MEAN to!"* I replied with *"Of course you didn't mean to. You're not an asshole going around breaking people's shit on purpose."*

Sometimes we intended harm and there is a whole other layer of accountability work to do there, but generally, we're just dumb humans bumbling around and fucking shit up even though we're trying out best. How different it would have gone if he had said *"Babe? I was trying to move your chiminea, and I broke it. I can try to fix it, but since it's clay it probably won't repair well enough to build fires in anymore. I'll replace it when I get paid on Friday."*

Just apologizing isn't enough, either. If an apology is called for, do it. But if you were the one stealing everyone's lunches at work, ceasing to steal those lunches isn't going to repair that trust. Think about how your actions or words impacted the other person, particularly if your actions were over a period of time. If you argue with your friend every time they tell you what they need from you, focus on listening instead. Make sure you hear and understand the nuts and bolts of their requests and commit them to memory.

Apologizing is a powerful tool for repairing relationships, but it isn't always appropriate. It may not be appropriate or safe to reach out. Or they may not be interested in what you have to say. If so, here's a new chance to respect their boundaries. This is something else that we should really consider on the regular when doing accountability work. In twelve-step language, we make amends unless doing so would cause the other person harm. And opening up someone's healed wounds for our own sense of well-being is definitely a form of harm.

A friend of mine really biffed his relationship a year ago and tried to reach out and apologize to his ex...who wasn't having it. He told me *"I need to respect her wanting to be left alone. It's the least I can do, right?"* Friend-person realized that this was not only a boundary, but his need to apologize was really about making *himself* feel better and less about repairing the harm he caused the woman in question.

If you think of someone you may have hurt in the past, what do you need to do to make sure it doesn't happen again in the future? It may be as simple as realizing *"I never thought about it that way. Now I know that 'convincing' someone is actually shitty and sketch and I'm over it."* Or it may mean, *"I really shouldn't drink that much, I'm far more likely to be a dick to other people when I do."* Here's a chance to make a commitment to yourself about your future interactions.

Beyond apologizing when needed and appropriate, it's always more powerful to show change and work for change instead of telling people that you have changed. Visible allyship and peer-to-peer support are critical to the kind of evolutionary change we desperately need to survive. Many recovery programs have people who have worked the program move into sponsorship roles, helping others in the ways they have been helped. Programs like The Forgiveness Project make public the work of accountability and healing. But it doesn't take renting a billboard. It may be volunteering time to a local advocacy group. Or demonstrating your accountability around others, therefore modeling interpersonal effectiveness as a mechanism of social change (ahhhh shit, I just got all political again, didn't I? #sorrynotsorry).

Questions to Consider

1) How, specifically, do you want to improve your respect for the boundaries of others? State this in positive and behaviorally focused terms, e.g. "I want to listen to the viewpoints of others without interrupting in order to understand where they are coming from" is far more doable than "I want to stop being a judgemental asshole."

2) What is your reason for wanting to make this improvement? What makes this a personal priority?

3) How will making these improvements change your life?

4) How are you hoping that these changes will improve life for people that you care about?

5) What are your best practices for moving forward? What are the actionable steps?

Conclusion

I want to tell you a little story.

My father is a person in long term recovery. He got sober through AA in the 1970s under the sponsorship of a grizzled old-timer from the Bill W. school of 12 step recovery. My father was also active duty military, so he took orders from his sponsor unblinkingly.

One day his sponsor was having him do knuckle push-ups.

Have you ever done them? Where the weight of the pushup goes into the knuckles of your hands instead of the flats of your palms? That shit HURTS, even if you are a military man in your mid-20s in fantastic shape.

My father did them, though. Complaining that they hurt. Asking if he could stop.

But every time he asked if he could stop, his sponsor told him to keep going.

Eventually, the pain got so bad, he jumped up and said "Fuck you! I don't have to do this!"

His sponsor slowly nodded his head in agreement and said "No shit."

That's it, isn't it? No matter what our past training and no matter the context of our current circumstances, we have the power to make choices that are the best for us and the world we want to live in.

What if we discussed our wants, needs, desires, and personal space as often and as matter-of-factly as we discuss football, movie star break-ups, and videogames? Our boundaries around these issues are something as real and tangible as our fingers and toes, and consent around these boundaries should be a given. What if the way we are doing it now is as useless and harmful as knuckle push-ups? If we all jumped up and said, "I don't have to do this anymore!" then the world would shift.

This book is a love letter to that idea. Because we all have so much capacity for healing. And healthy relationships. And we deserve safe passage in society.

But achieving this evolutionary shift requires such massive personal and societal change that it's hard not to feel hopeless, even as we sit here with bruised and bleeding knuckles.

If this book was as hard for you to read as it was for me to write, you are probably feeling overwhelmed as well. I don't write shallow, fluffy, feel-good books where emotional wellness work is over-simplified by burying it with mantras about how the laws of attraction will create instant happiness and success (not to mention perfect boundaries).

Problems that have existed for generations don't get fixed with platitudes, they get fixed when we do the difficult work of figuring out what we truly want in life, the kinds of relationships we want and don't want, and how we best communicate these desires to those around us while holding space for them to communicate their desires to us. You thought you got a book on boundaries and instead you got a manifesto on changing the world.

Same difference, though.

You can do this.

No shit.

Resources

Resources for Victims and Survivors of Interpersonal Violence

The National Domestic Violence Hotline – 1-800-799-7233 (SAFE) – www.ndvh.org
Speak to (or message) an advocate to seek immediate help, gain resources for survivors, or to discuss your options for leaving, should you choose to do so.

National Dating Abuse Helpline – 1-866-331-9474 – www.loveisrespect.org
Find ways to prevent or end an abusive relationship. This hotline is tailored to young people but offers resources for concerned friends and family, as well.

National Sexual Assault Hotline – 1-800-656-4673 (HOPE) – www.rainn.org
Provides strategies for prevention and safety as well as healing and recovery.

National Suicide Prevention Lifeline – 1-800-273-8255 (TALK) – www.suicidepreventionlifeline.org
Offers support to those in distress or crisis, and provides prevention resources for loved ones.

National Center for Victims of Crime – 1-855-484-2846 (VICTIM) – www.victimsofcrime.org
Comprehensive advocacy program that helps victims of crimes rebuild their lives.

National Human Trafficking Resource Center/Polaris Project – Call: 1-888-373-7888 – Text: HELP to BeFree (233733) – www.polarisproject.org
Call (or text) for crisis assistance, survivor support, or to report possible trafficking. This hotline can also connect you with local anti-trafficking services in your area.

National Network for Immigrant and Refugee Rights – 1-510-465-1984 – www.nnirr.org
An organization whose mission is to defend and expand rights for immigrants and refugees. Call for resources, and get connected to local allies.

National Coalition for the Homeless – 1-202-737-6444 – www.nationalhomeless.org
Network of advocacy groups working to prevent and end homelessness. Call to get emergency assistance from your local service providers.

National Resource Center on Domestic Violence – 1-800-537-2238 – www.nrcdv.org and www.vawnet.org
Call to request individualized and comprehensive technical assistance and resources on intervention and prevention strategies.

National Center on Domestic Violence, Trauma & Mental Health – 1-312-726-7020 ext. 2011 – www.nationalcenterdvtraumamh.org
Offers assistance, resources, and training to advocates and service providers working with survivors.

Resources Specific to Children

Childhelp USA/National Child Abuse Hotline – 1-800-422-4453 – www.childhelpusa.org
Call to get help in reporting child abuse or to speak to a Childhelp counselor.

Children's Defense Fund – 202-628-8787 – www.childrensdefense.org

A non-profit child advocacy program that lobbies for the rights of all children in America, particularly poor children, children of color and those with disabilities.

Child Welfare League of America – 202-688-4200 – www.cwla.org

Coalition of private and public agencies dedicated to serving vulnerable children and families

National Council on Juvenile and Family Court Judges – 775-507-4777 – www.ncjfcj.org

Child Protection and custody/resource center on domestic violence, which can benefit individuals who have been victims of coercive control.

Center for Judicial Excellence – 415-444-6556 – www.centerforjudicialexcellence.org

Nonprofit organization focused on creating judicial accountability in the family court system, their focus on policy change is a fantastic resource for individuals who have found that their experiences of coercive control were not considered crimes by the court system.

Resources Specific to Teens

Love Is Respect – Hotline: 1-866-331-9474 or Text: loveis to 22522 – www.loveisrespect.org

In association with the National Domestic Violence Hotline, this organization works to empower young people to prevent and end abusive relationships.

Break the Cycle – 202-849-6289 – www.breakthecycle.org

Organization centered around helping young people ages 12-24 build healthy and safe relationships.

Resource Specific to Deaf Women

Deaf Abused Women's Network (DAWN) – hotline@deafdawn.org – VP: 202-559-5366 – www.deafdawn.org

Agency that provides crisis intervention and survivor services for the Deaf, Hard of Hearing, and DeafBlind communities.

Resources Specific to Women of Color

Women of Color Network – 844-962-6462 – www.wocninc.org

A group established to address challenges facing Women of Color within the violence against women movement.

INCITE! Women of Color Against Violence – incite.natl@gmail.com – www.incite-national.org

Feminists of Color united to end state and domestic violence.

Resources to Specific to Latinx Individuals

Casa de Esperanza – Linea de crisis 24-horas/24-hour crisis line – 1-651-772-1611 – www.casadeesperanza.org

A bilingual domestic violence hotline. Their mission is to mobilize Latin@ communities to end domestic violence.

National Latin@ Network for Healthy Families and Communities – 1-651-646-5553 – www.nationallatinonetwork.org

Focuses on ending and preventing domestic violence in Latin@ communities, provides everything from shelter services to community engagement projects.

Resource Specific to Indigenous Women

National Indigenous Women's Resource Center – 855-649-7299 – www.niwrc.org

Organization dedicated to ending violence amongst native and indigenous populations through education and policy development.

Resources Specific to Asian and Pacific Islander Individuals

Asian and Pacific Islander Institute on Domestic Violence – 415-568-3315 – www.apiidv.org

Resource center for Asian and Pacific Islander communities facing issues of domestic violence.

Committee Against Anti-Asian Violence (CAAAV) – 1-212-473-6485 – www.caaav.org

Committee centered around organizing Asian communities to fight for institutional change.

Manavi – 1-732-435-1414 – www.manavi.org

Meeting needs (both immediate and long-term) for South Asian Women affected by violence.

Resource Specific to African-American Individuals

National Center on Violence Against Women in the Black Community – 1-844-778-5462 – ujimacommunity.org

Provides resources to and advocates for the Black Community in response to domestic, sexual, and community violence.

Resources Specific to Lesbian, Gay, Plurisexual, Trans, and NonBinary Individuals

The Audre Lorde Project – 1-718-596-0342 – www.alp.org

Organization working towards community wellness and social/economic justice for Lesbian, Gay, Bisexual, Two-Spirit, Trans and Gender Non Conforming People of Color.

LGBT National Help Center – 1-206-350-4283 – www.glnh.org

Provides peer support and local resources to the LGBT community.

National Gay and Lesbian Task Force – 1-202-393-5177 – www.ngltf.org

Organization focused on advancing justice and equality for LGBTQ people.

Northwest Network of Bisexual, Trans, Lesbian & Gay Survivors of Abuse – 1-206-568-7777 – www.nwnetwork.org

Network offering direct resources for victims of abuse, as well as resources for advocacy organizations.

Trans Lifeline – 877-565-8860 – www.translifeline.org

A hotline dedicated to improving the quality of trans lives and ending the epidemic of trans suicide by offering justice-oriented community aid.

Trevor Project – 1-866-488-7386 – thetrevorproject.org

Focused on preventing suicide and crisis intervention for LGBTQ and questioning individuals. The hotline is dedicated to helping those in need of immediate help.

It Gets Better – info@itgetsbetter.org – itgetsbetter.org

Aiming to uplift, empower and connect LGBTQ youth around the world.

Resource Specific to Older Adults

National Clearinghouse on Abuse in Later Life – 1-608-255-0539 – www.ncall.us

Provides technical assistance, training, and resources in order to advocate for elderly victims of abuse.

Resource Specific to Men

1in6 – 1in6.org
Provides men affected by sexual abuse or assault with survivor's resources.

Legal Resources

Battered Women's Justice Project – 1-800-903-0111 – www.bwjp.org
National resource center on civil and criminal justice responses to intimate partner violence.

Legal Momentum – 1-212-925-6635 – www.legalmomentum.org
Provides expert legal council in order to ensure economic and personal security for women and girls.

WomensLaw.org – www.womenslaw.org
Provides relevant legal information for all genders in regards to domestic and sexual violence.

National Clearinghouse for the Defense of Battered Women – 1-800-903-0111 x 3 – www.ncdbw.org
Provides customized technical assistance to victims of battery who are facing criminal charges or serving prison sentences.

Legal Network for Gender Equity – (202) 588-5180 – nwlc.org/join-the-legal-network/
Seeks gender justice in a variety of ways; in courtrooms, through public policies and cultural changes.

Resources Specific to Violence Prevention

National Organization for Men Against Sexism (NOMAS) – 1-720-466-3882 – www.nomas.org
A Call to Men – 1-917-922-6738 – www.acalltomen.org
Men Can Stop Rape – 1-202-265-6530 – www.mencanstoprape.org
Men Stopping Violence – 1-866-717-9317 – www.menstoppingviolence.org

Media Resources (Books, Websites, Etc.)

Learning Good Consent: Building Ethical Relationships In A Complicated World – Cindy Crabb
Empowered Boundaries: Setting Boundaries and Inspiring Social Change – Cristien Storm
Invisible Chains: Overcoming Coercive Control In Your Intimate Relationship – Lisa Aronson Fontes
Conflict Is Not Abuse – Sarah Schulman
Dare To Lead – Brene Brown
The Gift of Fear – Gavin DeBecker
Betty Martin's "Wheel of Consent" and "The Three Minute Game" - *Betty Martin.org*
How to Put Together a Consent Workshop – *https://tinyurl.com/ConsentWorkshopZine*
I Heart Consent Workshop Facilitator Guide – *https://tinyurl.com/IHeartConsentManual*

References

2015 U.S. Transgender Survey Report. (n.d.). Retrieved from https://vawnet.org/material/2015-us-transgender-survey-report

Aravind VK, Krishnaram VD, Thasneem Z. Boundary crossings and violations in clinical settings. *Indian J Psychol Med.* 2012;34(1):21–24. doi:10.4103/0253-7176.96151

Breit, S., Kupferberg, A., Rogler, G., & Hasler, G. (2018). Vagus Nerve as Modulator of the Brain-Gut Axis in Psychiatric and Inflammatory Disorders. *Frontiers in psychiatry, 9,* 44. doi:10.3389/fpsyt.2018.00044

Boas, F. (1997). *Handbook of American Indian languages: Franz Boas.* London: Routledge/Thoemmes.

Bottalico, B. (2009). Neuroscience, accountability and individual boundaries. *Frontiers in Human Neuroscience, 3.* doi:10.3389/neuro.09.045.2009

Carlson, K. (n.d.). Consent Statement Summary. Retrieved from https://www.ncsfreedom.org/component/k2/item/784

Carlson, K. (n.d.). Consent Counts Statement. Retrieved from https://www.ncsfreedom.org/component/k2/item/782

Chapman, S., & Routledge, C. (2005). *Key thinkers in linguistics and the philosophy of language.* Edinburgh: Edinburgh University Press.

Chödrön, P., & Sell, E. H. (2018). *Comfortable with uncertainty: 108 teachings.* Boulder: Shambhala.

Chödrön, P. (2018, November 23). How We Get Hooked By Shenpa -- Pema Chödrön. Retrieved from https://www.lionsroar.com/how-we-get-hooked-shenpa-and-how-we-get-unhooked/

Crabb, C. (2017). *Learning good consent.* Microcosm Publishing.

DeBecker, G. (2000). *The gift of fear.* London: Bloomsbury.

Dutton, M. A., Goodman, L., & Schmidt, R. J. (2008). Development and Validation of a Coercive Control Measure for Intimate Partner Violence in Boston, Massachusetts and Washington, DC, 2004. *ICPSR Data Holdings.* doi:10.3886/icpsr04570

Edwards, S. R., Bradshaw, K. A., & Hinsz, V. B. (2014). Denying Rape but Endorsing Forceful Intercourse: Exploring Differences Among Responders. *Violence and Gender, 1*(4), 188-193. doi:10.1089/vio.2014.0022

Fontes, L. A. (2015). *Invisible chains: Overcoming coercive control in your intimate relationship.* New York, NY: Guilford Press.

FORGE Empowering. Healing. Connecting. (n.d.). Retrieved from https://forge-forward.org/2013/04/06/power-and-control-tactics/

Gender Differences in Heterosexual College Students' Conceptualizations and Indicators of Sexual Consent: Implications for Contemporary Sexual Assault Prevention Education. (n.d.). Retrieved from https://www.tandfonline.com/doi/full/10.1080/00224499.2013.792326?scroll=top&needAccess=true&

Get Statistics. (n.d.). Retrieved from https://www.nsvrc.org/node/4737

Hatch, L. (2014, January 16). How to Respond to Boundary Violations: Do's and Don'ts. Retrieved from https://blogs.psychcentral.com/sex-addiction/2013/12/how-to-respond-to-boundary-violations-dos-and-donts/

Hemmendinger, D. (2013, April 23). Data compression. Retrieved from https://www.britannica.com/technology/data-compression

Hunter, M. (2007, June 22). How To Write A BIFF Response. Retrieved from https://www.highconflictinstitute.com/free-articles/2018/1/12/how-to-write-a-biff-response

Jenkins, A. (2001). *Invitations to responsibility: The therapeutic engagement of men who are violent and abusive.* Adelaide: Dulwich Centre Publications.

Kitzinger, C., & Frith, H. (n.d.). Just Say No? The Use of Conversation Analysis in Developing a Feminist Perspective on Sexual Refusal - CELIA KITZINGER, HANNAH FRITH, 1999. Retrieved from https://journals.sagepub.com/doi/abs/10.1177/0957926599010003002

Kennedy, L. P. (n.d.). What Is Coercive Control in an Abusive Relationship? Retrieved from https://www.webmd.com/women/features/what-is-coercive-control#1

Lorde, A. (2007). *Sister outsider: Essays and speeches.* New York: Crossing Press.

Lovefraud. (2019, May 15). 8 ways your body warns you about sociopaths. Retrieved from https://lovefraud.com/7-ways-your-body-warns-you-about-sociopaths/

Markowsky, G. (2017, June 16). Information theory. Retrieved from https://www.britannica.com/science/information-theory/Physiology

McGuire, L. (2018, October 19). A Short History of Sexual Consent. Retrieved from https://www.kinkly.com/a-short-history-of-sexual-consent/2/17399

Mirk, S. (2017). *Sex from scratch: Making your own relationship rules.* Portland, OR: Microcosm Publishing.

"Monoaminergic." Monoaminergic - an Overview | ScienceDirect Topics, www.sciencedirect.com/topics/biochemistry-genetics-and-molecular-biology/monoaminergic.

Mythcommunication: It's Not That They Don't Understand, They Just Don't Like The Answer. (2011, March 21). Retrieved from https://yesmeansyesblog.wordpress.com/2011/03/21/mythcommunication-its-not-that-they-dont-understand-they-just-dont-like-the-answer/

Neff, K., & Germer, C. K. (2018). *The mindful self-compassion workbook: A proven way to accept yourself, build inner strength, and thrive.* New York, NY: Guilford Press.

New Research Explores Our Personal Sense of Space." Monitor on Psychology, American Psychological Association, Dec. 2009, www.apa.org/monitor/2009/12/space.

Ng, Wee Keong, et al. "Lossless and Lossy Data Compression." Evolutionary Algorithms in Engineering Applications, 1997, pp. 173–188., doi:10.1007/978-3-662-03423-1_10.

Office for the Prevention of Domestic Violence. (n.d.). Retrieved from https://www.opdv.ny.gov/professionals/abusers/coercivecontrol.html

O'Shea, T. (2011) *Green Paper Report: Consent in History, Theory and Practice*. Essex Autonomy Project: https://autonomy.essex.ac.uk/wp-content/uploads/2016/11/Consent-GPR-June-2012.pdf

Rape Culture. (n.d.). Retrieved from https://www.csbsju.edu/chp/health-promotion/sexual-violence/rape-culture

Rockwell, I. N. (2002). *The five wisdom energies: A Buddhist way of understanding personalities, emotions, and relationships*. Boston: Shambhala.

Schulman, S. (2017). *Conflict is not abuse: Overstating harm, community responsibility and the duty of repair*. Vancouver: Arsenal Pulp Press.

Shepherd, B. (2019, January 31). How a simple tool called the 'No Test' could help identify a potentially abusive partner. Retrieved from https://www.abc.net.au/news/2019-01-31/how-the-no-test-could-help-prevent-domestic-violence/10764100?fbclid=IwAR0Fz_xmBurqGwIqz4WsEu-93kxv8ZKK_tJv3nzfB4aRHuoGWdQCdIh7YxM&pfmredir=sm&sf206928305=1

Skene, L., & Smallwood, R. (2002, January 05). Informed consent: Lessons from Australia. Retrieved from https://www.bmj.com/content/324/7328/39.long

Skylar. (2018, November 19). The Gray Rock Method of Dealing With Psychopaths. Retrieved from https://180rule.com/the-gray-rock-method-of-dealing-with-psychopaths/

Stark, E. (2009). Rethinking Coercive Control. Violence Against Women, 15(12), 1509–1525. https://doi.org/10.1177/1077801209347452

Stark, E. D. (2009). *Coercive control: The entrapment of women in personal life*. Oxford: Oxford University Press.

Storm, C. (2018). *Empowered boundaries: Speaking truth, setting boundaries, and inspiring social change*. Berkeley, CA: North Atlantic Books.

The History Behind Sexual Consent Policies. (2014, October 05). Retrieved from https://www.npr.org/2014/10/05/353922015/the-history-behind-sexual-consent-policies

Thelilynews. (2019, February 14). It's not enough to hope for the best. Millennials are writing contracts for their relationships. - The Lily. Retrieved from https://www.thelily.com/its-not-enough-to-hope-for-the-best-millennials-are-writing-contracts-for-their-relationships/

Trans-Specific Power and Control Tactics. (n.d.). Retrieved from https://vawnet.org/material/trans-specific-power-and-control-tactics

Violence Against Trans and Non-Binary People. (n.d.). Retrieved from https://vawnet.org/sc/serving-trans-and-non-binary-survivors-domestic-and-sexual-violence/violence-against-trans-and

"Visceral Influences on Brain and Behavior." Neuron, Cell Press, 20 Feb. 2013, www.sciencedirect.com/science/article/pii/S0896627313001402.

Vrangalova, Z. (2018, November 02). Everything You Need to Know About Consent That You Never Learned in Sex Ed. Retrieved from https://www.teenvogue.com/story/consent-how-to

What is Rape Culture? - Definition from Kinkly. (n.d.). Retrieved from https://www.kinkly.com/definition/14736/rape-culture

SUBSCRIBE TO EVERYTHING WE PUBLISH!

Do you love what Microcosm publishes?

Do you want us to publish more great stuff?

Would you like to receive each new title as it's published?

Subscribe as a BFF to our new titles and we'll mail them all to you as they are released!

$13-30/mo, pay what you can afford!

microcosmpublishing.com/bff

...AND HELP US GROW YOUR SMALL WORLD!

More Five Minute Therapy:

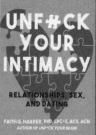